How to Implement the Computerized Quality Management System

A Quality by Delitala Book
Part 4

By: Michael A. Delitala

Dedicated to Ben Riblett. The best project manager there will ever be to implement a QMS.

Copyrights

Contents

Chapter 1
Introduction

I'm Michael A. Delitala, the author of The Revisionist and Quality by Delitala (QbD) series.

Last year (2024) in August, I formed the Delitala Quality Consulting & Author Corporation.

It marked my formal exit from Corporate America (as a W-2 employee, for clarity).

Since then, I've completed a few consulting gigs. I have also authored fourteen books. Thirteen of which are published and are available on Amazon. The remaining are in-process and will be published one per week through the end of 2025.

To be honest with you, I'll have three more of The Revisionist series and potentially eighty-six more volumes of Quality by Delitala. Yes, I have a lot to say about Quality.

Listen. I'm going to be bold in this volume. That said, I'm not trying to be too provocative. So, please keep that in mind.

All over my LinkedIn thread, there are people just like me. Eliminated from a position due to some restructuring so that the company can be profitable, they're super smart, remarkably experienced, yet unable to land the next job. This does not make sense.

In my case, I've been a Project Lead and Business Lead to implement a new computerized quality management system at multiple large and small pharmaceutical firms.

In my most recent experience, it was Veeva. I've also implemented Digital Trackwise, Trackwise On-Premise, and specific modules of SAP. I've even implemented an artificially intelligent deviation trending tool. I've also participated in greater than 30 years of improvements or upgrades to Agile-QMS, Pilgrim-QMS, Sparta, and GxPLearn. I hope this informs you that I am qualified to write about this subject.

The most advanced quality management system that I have ever worked with was at Emergent BioSolutions (Lansing, MI). Emergent implemented all modules in SAP. And they were smart enough not to over configure it which is usually the natural tendency at larger pharma companies (which is why it costs a firm so much money – if they went with an out of the box solution, SAP is actually very cheap compared to other computerized QMSs).

It was beautiful! A work of art. Listen. In most pharma companies, the computerized QMS is disjointed. Modules are disparate and in most cases are in unique applications. This cost firms an excessive amount of money because it relies heavily on individual's manual performance in each application, and there is an extensive amount of training and retraining required to gain access to multiple platforms. This is very expensive. When I was at Kite, I estimated that the amount of training I was putting on cost in excess of $1,000,000 annually just at the corporate site. Multiply that by six additional manufacturing plants who have a lot more staff to keep trained than a HQ site!

At Emergent, literally everything was in SAP and the beauty of it being all in SAP was that all modules communicated with each other. Therefore, with the simple push of a button, a Quality dispositioner could see that a batch was ready to be dispositioned in that all deviations were closed, all change controls were at the right status and so on and so forth. That's how it's supposed to work! (and it's very cost effective).

Anyway, there are a plethora of open positions in this space, especially with Veeva.

Which is a great place to work. Amazing supervisors. Excellent benefits. Fantastic culture.

I think I might have applied for 6 or 7 positions. All of which I'm qualified for, and my resume is almost line by line, bullet by bullet, and nearly identical to the job posting.

Yet, for some reason, I receive near-immediate rejection letters. I've even guerilla war fared it and reached out to my extensive Veeva network, who say, "hey man, we've sent your resume upward to the hiring manager and to HR". Yet, there are still no calls. No interviews.

I have this peculiar feeling that because I've become self-employed, and a prolific author, that I'm no longer employable by Corporate America (as a W-2 employee, for clarity). Particularly in the areas that I'm actually an expert at such as implementing eQMSs.

How bizarre is that! I often say this out loud: "I feel like I'm in Bizzarro world!"

Here's what I think is going on:

My resume doesn't pass muster with the AI bots screening it. Why? I don't know.

Veeva is all over my resume. I mean, it was a project I led for four years at one of the largest pharmaceutical companies on planet Earth. (and we landed it on time, under budget and right first time which is unheard of!). The only red flag on my resume is that I was only at Avidity for eight months. That's a long story in and of itself and is only for conversation!

Perhaps the Hiring Managers don't really know what they're looking for.

Listen up Hiring Managers: Today, all of us older folks all we care about is having a good supervisor, enjoying the work, and being valued by the company we work for. It's super simple. We just want to know that you appreciate our hard work. We don't care about rank any longer and these days, any amount of money is good. (Seriously, it's pathetic!)

Or, the reality is, that the company does not want to pay a huge salary for Quality staff members. When I left Corporate America, I was an Associate Director (which means just barely "executive") and I was making $200,000 as my base salary, and when you combine benefits, bonus, 401k etc, I was making close to $500,000 per year. That is a shit ton of money. Companies are smarter now. They realize they can pay today's inexperienced generation a hell of a lot less and not care so much about having to hold their hand to get them through their day.

It's unfortunate, but it makes sense.

Well, Trackwise and Veeva, listen up.

You want talent to join your team? (without having to micromanage today's workforce?)

There's a whole bunch of us old folks without a job. That means we'll take less of a salary and we'll run circles around your hired younger generations. (and we won't complain that you're holding us to a due date or a timeline!)

Finally, and you'll hate me for this, but since you won't hire me, I don't really care, this book, "Quality by Delitala Volume 14 – How to Implement the Computerized Quality Management System" goes into explicit detail on how to implement Veeva. It will be a step-by-step guide detailing all the industry secrets and steps for how to implement the computerized QMS. I say it's specific to Veeva but the reality is this is how you implement any computerized GMP system.

This will be my QbD masterpiece.

There's only one way to stop me from selling it.

Hire me (as a consultant for that dream job where you want someone to "evangelize" how great Veeva is). Because, as of this writing, there are 354 open Veeva positions and I've applied to seven of them. One of them has the lowest salary I've considered since the year 2000.

All pharma companies will want this volume.

Well, better said, they'll need it since Veeva is taking the industry by storm.

Thank you for your interest in Veeva Inbox ×

Veeva Systems <no-reply@hire.lever.co>
to me ▾

veeva

DO THE RIGHT THING | CUSTOMER SUCCESS | EMPLOYEE SUCCESS | SPEED

Hi Michael,

Thank you for your interest in Veeva and for giving us the opportunity to review your application for the Business Consultant - Life Sciences Quality position.

After reviewing your resume, we've made the decision to not move forward at this time.

We appreciate your interest in Veeva and wish you success in your job search.

Kind regards,

Veeva Talent Attraction Team

For future opportunities visit our career site: https://careers.veeva.com/

Chapter 2
Additional Context Leading Into the "How-To"

This book will not be about how to select your new computerized QMS. That could be another volume, but honestly that topic bores me. Here's why: It doesn't actually matter what the masses think. It only matters what the Head of Quality, Head of IT, and their counterparts think. I'm very sorry. And it's the truth.

In my last year at Amgen, Leadership made a decision. We're either upgrading our current Trackwise On-Premise to Digital Trackwise, we're implementing Veeva-QMS, or a hybrid approach where we will improve our current On-Premise Trackwise. The two companies arrived, made their pitch, and the whole of the team felt completely underwhelmed. Veeva-QMS seemed clunky at best and we wanted a simplified experience for our Users. Digital Trackwise, at this point in time, was a mirror image of the On-Premise version and we gave Sparta a lot of adverse feedback to that end.

We made a cost-effective decision to keep what we had (On-Premise Trackwise) yet we were going to streamline, and improve it based on Customer User Requirements and their Preferences. That said, in the background, my super smart quality supervisor decided that as a Thousand Oaks Site, that we were going to do our own thing. I felt conflicted about this at the time, but as time went on, I realized how brilliant a strategy it was.

We hired this unknown QMS company from Turkey. They were IT geniuses that could bring to life modules in quality by writing the code and implementing it right in front of us in real time. We were blown away. So, we hunkered down, and we used Design Thinking principles to reimagine the quality management system. There were no limits. And Quality by Delitala (AKA the Mike Thing as defined in QbD Book 4) was in full effect. I created amazing process flow diagrams in seconds representing how I wanted the full of the QMS to be integrated and speaking to each other. (Just like the SAP version at Emergent BioSolutions).

In a few short but fast weeks, we had the QMS of our dreams. It was at about this moment in time, the Head of Quality learned of what we were doing and told us, "Radical idea but we're an enterprise company and there is no way in hell I will let you implement a stand-alone version of the QMS". Obviously, we were crushed. Because even though at first, I was not all in, I recognized after some deep conversations with my supervisor how we could come out as rock-stars. And in the end, that's exactly what happened.

We showcased our stand-alone quality management system to the C-Suite Executive team as well as all of the Corporate Global Program Owners of the QMS and they ooo'd and awed at how remarkably simple it was to use and how integrated it was. It was exactly how it was always intended to be, and it was the most compliant QMS anyone had ever laid eyes upon. Simplicity breeds compliance.

Not too long after this demonstration an edict came down from the Head Cheese of Quality that it was time to simplify our On-Premise trackwise. We were given a budget and eight weeks to completely revolutionize the quality management system. If you've read any of my previous volumes you'll recognize immediately that 1) this is impossible and 2) change is dynamic and will be abhorred and mutinied by the masses. Except this time, leadership actually took a top-down approach and all that were involved felt supported, hunkered down, did the work, and only the newest, least experienced employees complained, and no one cared about them (sorry, just being honest). And in eight very long weeks, we had our new and improved QMS.

That's not the only thing that happened though. Sparta was devastated by our feedback and by our decision. They used this decision to review our feedback in detail. Fast forward to another year. I'm now at Gilead / Kite. It's my first week on the job and my supervisor sends me from Santa Monica, CA to Foster City, CA to participate in a week-long workshop to receive demonstrations again from Sparta and Veeva so that Gilead Leadership can decide on which QMS to implement.

At the time, Gilead is using On-Premise Trackwise. I was able to see what they're using and to be honest, it was the most advanced version of Trackwise I had ever witnessed. It was amazing. It was integrated with itself, and it was a work of art. To this day, I still have no idea why Gilead wanted to change to a different QMS. They didn't know either! What I came to understand was that Gilead just likes to spend money every three to five years in implementing some new computerized system.

Kite was using Agile-QMS (an Oracle application) which they received for free while they were still clinical. I was the quality owner of it, and I made my own share of improvements to the system, but it was so antiquated that I used to joke with my colleagues that it reminded me of an AOL-chat room. I hope you're laughing. At the same time, I found some of its features to be quite eloquent because they were so simple to use. In short though, it was limited, and Agile themselves told us that they could no longer support the version we were using because they could not maintain its validated status. (I can't even make this stuff up!) My IT partner and I had to write many deviations and change controls to support the system being in a sustainment mode and so it would be somewhat defensible to Regulators. We only had to defend it once and we were lucky to get out of that inspection relatively unscathed and without a Regulatory Observation. In any regard, I'm conveying that we had a business case to make change vs Gilead's position.

Sparta was first to make the pitch. I was busy building relationships and introducing myself to all of my new colleagues prior to the pitch. And one thing I told everyone that I met was "be prepared to be underwhelmed by Digital Trackwise. You know, I just sat through all of these demonstrations having just come from Amgen". And then they presented. And all of us were blown away. They had really listened to the feedback provided by us at Amgen and completely overhauled the system. It was modular. It had artificial intelligence so that you could push a button and trend deviations right on the spot. And it was integrated. It was beautiful. It blew me away.

Compared to Veeva, which was still clunky, Digital Trackwise stole the show. Our Leadership had set up a process by which we'd each pen our own notes, execute Process Exercises in each module, and then overall rank which system we wanted. It was truly a democratic process until it was not. What we in the audience did not know where the financial terms of either system. Digital Trackwise was to cost $1,000,000 to implement the full QMS (in one year) with $1,000,000 to maintain it year over year. Relatively speaking for a QMS, that's cheap! Veeva was going to cost $18,000,000 (over four years) to implement, with a $2,000,000 maintenance fee year over year. Are you kidding me!!? Also, there's something that everyone who wants to implement Veeva needs to know. Veeva shuts the system down three times per year in order to implement patches, upgrades, and new products for the system. These shutdowns can last as little as 24 consecutive hours, or as long as seven calendar days. What it also means is that the full of the system is down. Everything. Deviation, Document Control, disposition, it all shuts down during this time. This has a huge impact on the business and finance (the bottom line!). Batches cannot be electronically dispositioned during these down times. Versus Digital Trackwise, where they take a module-by-module shutdown approach ensuring business continuity. Just saying. Also, keep in mind that at this time, Gilead had turned on the Document Control module in Veeva.

All of the voting ends. The results are tallied. And it's a landslide victory for Digital Trackwise. A few weeks go by and the Leadership announces the decision that Veeva is the chosen one. 1) We already have Document Control there and we do not want multiple systems (even though they can be integrated) and 2) IT will own the system and IT likes the way Veeva works versus Digital Trackwise. Let's take a few moments of silence on this decision. What are you going to do? One must support the decisions of the leadership (even when their decisions make no sense).

There is one more important note to make here for additional context and it's a huge proactive lesson to learn while considering what QMS computerized system to implement. **The company must know its identity.** In this case, I'm being specific about the kind of products the company makes. I'm not certain, but I do believe that the situation between Kite and Gilead was quite unique relative to their products and therefore their business model. Kite is an immunotherapy company and follows the regulations of drug substance biologics. Gilead is mostly a small-molecule drug product company with a smattering of drug substance biologics and some medical device combo products. In addition, Kite is mostly an insourced model of manufacturing where Gilead is mostly an outsourced model of manufacturing. Also, there's the whole GCP space to consider where their QMS is largely a representation of clinical trial data and a completely different model than the two aforementioned GMP models. These are critical points because they were trying to implement one Enterprise Computerized QMS and as a team, we had to understand our differences and relate them to relevant and applicable regulations and business models.

You might be thinking, "Hey Mike, it's all the same at the end of the day". It's actually not. There are unique aspects to Immunotherapy that one must consider for their QMS. For example, most companies do not allow product to be dispositioned as released when it does not meet specification. In Immunotherapy, Regulators expect out-of-specification product to still be provided back to the patient. This is because these are very sick individuals who need their still viable cells given back to them so they can remain somewhat healthy. Well, your QMS needs to account for this. There are many other unique aspects, so I highlight just one for this illustration. The point is, **the parent and child companies need to be put in a position to understand these differences in order to create user requirements that are applicable to the full of the Enterprise.**

And then in my experiences as the Project Lead and Business Lead, one must always be prepared to bring to the table the constant reminder about intra-company differences so that all parties involved have all of their user requirements met in order to be compliant to law and internal standards, towards the full end of truly having an aligned enterprise computerized QMS.

Chapter 3
A Core Team Must Establish Project Guiding Principles

… and remain focused on what the business drivers are to have a modern QMS.

Guiding Principles keep the team honest and the project on track. It is very easy to go off track in project meetings because departments and informed stakeholders all want what they want. And usually, it's based on past experiences. Well, if you truly want a modern QMS, then the past is the past and the system is the future so focus on what is possible versus what perhaps may be an antiquated way of thinking. Also, it's important to have a safe word during all project meetings. The name of the project that serves as the inspiration for this volume was "Next Gen QMS". It also became our meeting safe word. If we felt we were way off the agenda or if a discussion was spiraling and going in circles, then a Business Lead or a Project Lead could utter the safe word. Upon such an utterance the Project Lead would table the conversation and take action to set up a specific meeting to resolve the topic.

Below are example vision and guiding principle statements. It is paramount that every once in a while, these are flashed up and discussed in a meeting. Also, it should be obvious that the full core team must agree to the vision and principles. I speak more about what a "core team" is in the next chapter.

The Future is Now

The Vision
- A simple, enterprise globally facing and integrated system that is user focused, enables data driven insights for focused decisions, and adaptable to the ever-evolving needs of the business.

Guiding Principles
- Keep it **SIMPLE** to achieve scalability and compliance
- Focus on **USER EXPERIENCE**, fit for purpose and ease of use
- Design for **AGILITY** and **ADAPTABILITY** to evolving business needs
- Be **BOLD** and **INNOVATIVE** with the future in mind
- Focus on use of **DATA TO DRIVE INSIGHTS** in the vein of continuous improvement
- **ENTERPRISE & ALIGNMENT MINDSETS**

At the start of this volume, I indicated I would not be providing any details on how to select your computerized QMS. And I will hold true to that statement. However, the company must know their identity and they must understand what is driving the need to want to implement a new computerized QMS. Below are some primary business drivers in glorious marketing format for your consideration and review. There are other drives but to me, these stand out as the most important.

Primary Business Drivers for a Modern QMS

Functionality
- Support evolving QMS needs by replacing legacy systems which are complex, inflexible and at end-of-life.

Information Connectivity
- Integrated systems improve efficiency by connecting product, regulatory, and quality information.

Knowledge & Intelligence
- Leverage "deep learning" to identify risks that are not easily identified. Real time data visualization.

Usability
- Simple and intuitive user interface to improve the user experience.

Process Automation
- Reduce repetitive data entry, manual steps, and inefficiencies through automation.

External Access & Collaboration
- Contract partners can directly enter data and collaborate with Company to address various quality event workstreams.

Just-in-Time Training
- Expanded use of just-in-time training and digital adoption tools to ensure targeted training to users.

Chapter 4
Next, You Build a Team and Onboard Them

I am going to be honest. In creating content for this volume, I find myself wavering back and forth in how it all should or could be set up. With that in mind, I'm going to write the chapters in the order that I actually led the project. I think it will create a nice flow and then by the end of this volume, all of the parts and pieces will make up the full of the puzzle that is the how to implement the computerized QMS. With that in mind, this chapter intends to describe how to dig into the historical perspective, how to complete a data review leading to data insights, the decision making model, defining roles and responsibilities, and other items all of which go into a massive marketing presentation so that you may onboard a team while simultaneously creating content that will be used to keep leaders informed and users interested in what's in it for them. Onboarding the team is paramount to your success as the Project Lead and the Business Lead.

Yes, this is another Mike Thing. My leadership did not find value in the Mike Thing until the middle of the phase 2 of our project where I was called into a meeting with the highest level of leaders and my name was thrown in the mud (full name repeated 10 times as in "Mike Delitala this, Mike Delitala that") where I was accused of ignoring our users. It was a horrible experience, but I'll go into that in another chapter. I hope this grabs your attention and re-engages your interest into why onboarding the team with massive amounts of marketing materials is necessary for the success of your leadership and the project. It's not easy. Communication ended up being the most critical of all attributes. I'll go into that later.

Regarding historical perspective…

I hate to be cliché, but the adage applies here; those who do not know the past are doomed to repeat it. I take pride in the fact that I was one of the first corporate guys to join Kite in the corporate space. When I joined as the Deviation/CAPA Global Program Owner, we had just become commercial. That's a critical point to make in understanding the maturity of an organization who was becoming very large very fast. What it means is that the quality programs, all of them, were immature relative to the phase of the product Kite was now in. That equates to the concept that the records being documented in the QMS were also immature. Better said, not up to the commercial standard that a Regulator would expect. Therefore, understanding this as part of the historical perspective makes your job as a Program Manager and Business Project Lead even more taxing; knowing you have to mature the QMS while implementing a new QMS. I'm very proud of doing both, but it was the most difficult charge of my career. (The most rewarding too!)

Let's be a bit more succinct.

Understanding historical perspective is critical in that one will know what was implemented in the past and why. Therefore, you are not doomed to repeat it. What needs to be implemented in the future, and why. Therefore, you are committed to the User, the business, and most importantly, compliance to regulations. And the overarching theme in this use case is how to align with the Parent company in as best as possible while highlighting critical differences towards the end of a unified, aligned, enterprise computerized QMS. In the end, all of that must coalesce, and if it does, then, and only then can it be successful.

Here were some items that I reviewed while assessing the historical perspective:

Item Evaluated	Why?	What I Learned...
Timeframe the company was Clinical	Regulatory Bodies expect companies to have a phase appropriate framework. The lower the phase, the lower the rigor. The higher the phase, the higher the rigor leading into being Commercial.	• Why we implemented Agile-QMS – It was free – to save on the cost of Quality. • Agile-QMS was implemented as an out of the box solution (no configuration). Therefore, it met the minimum regulatory requirements.
The actual date that the company became commercial	Commercial companies are expected to be fully compliant to the applicable regulations for their product, facility, and with ICHQ10.	• The QMS (the full program – Policy, procedures, and computerized system) needed a full overhaul. It all served its purpose while being clinical, but there was a long road ahead to being up to a commercial standard. This helped me plan better for the future. • This date is also the line of demarcation. Anything before this line is clinical and it's okay if the data is not totally compliant to a commercial standard. Anything after this line and effort should be completed towards evaluating it for compliance and mitigating any noncompliance.

How many sites are commercial, how many are clinical, how many are planned to become commercial and are there any sites where this is not applicable?	This is just the start of understanding the business complexities of what you're about to face while trying to implement a globally facing enterprise computerized QMS.	<ul><li>N/A for the HQ Site</li><li>2 Sites were commercial.</li><li>1 Site was about to be commercial.</li><li>2 Sites had a way to go to being commercial.</li><li>1 site would forever remain clinical.</li></ul>
Internal Audit Observations & Responses	Specifically, to understand if any element or aspect of the quality management system had received any internal audit observations.	<ul><li>The internal audit program was quite rigorous (which was a good thing) and the full of the QMS had many internal audit observations.</li><li>There were also a lot of CAPAs from Internal Audits that had planned to change the QMS across seven locations. That said, it was not within their power to change any of the QMS and what I ended up having to do was form a committee with the VP of Compliance so that we could document our decisions on to move forward or not move forward. After that, I implemented a QMS governance board so that all could still feel like they were heard even if I had to say "no" without actually saying "no" (and yes, that's another Mike Thing".)</li></ul>
Comprehensive Regulatory Inspection Outcomes	Specifically, to understand if any element or aspect of the quality management system had received any inspectional observations.	<ul><li>There was one observation made by the IGJ (Dutch) on the Deviation Management Program. This is important because you have to make a decision on whether you'll incorporate the corrective action to that observation in the new QMS or if you'll write a justification for not including it. In my case, I convinced the VP of Compliance to justify not having it in which we recorded it in the change control governing the project.</li></ul>

	This is simply due diligence. • At some point during the implementation, you may have some doomsdayers or naysayers who abhor change and they might refuse to move to the new QMS. So, if you have these details in your back pocket, it becomes relatively easy to convince a department head or stubborn Head of Quality that it will in fact be in their best interests to join the rest of the organization. It sounds something like this: "Sure, Head of Quality, you can keep the current Agile-QMS. However, you'll have to take on the cost of it in your budget. It's currently XYZ amount of dollars per year. Please let me know when you have an approved budget and I will be happy to write a change control that documents the transition to your budget code. "By the way, Gilead is taking on the full cost of the Veeva-QMS year over year for all time".	
Existing Contract and cost of the current QMS		• We had a limited amount of time to renew the contract and for the last time we would have to renew it at the cost of $150,000. • The cost of maintaining it in sustainment mode was greater than $1,000,000 when we factored in all of the IT support, the IT tickets, the QMS Records, and the amount of time for each team within QMS Records.

	• Existing costs shall also include the number of deviations, number of CAPAs, and number of change controls created in order to keep the system defensible to regulators.	
All QMS past changes and the justification for those changes	• In the beginning of this chapter, we discussed not repeating the past. If it was changed, then it is critical to understand what was changed and why it was changed so that as the Leader, you're not inadvertently changing it back and recreating a problem that was fixed an eon ago. (This is the comedy of the full circle of quality life that I describe in detail in QbD V4).	• A lot. I created a log of past changes with their justifications to help speed up the User Requirements Gathering process and to remind Users of the already great work they had completed previously.

| Past workshop proposed changes to the QMS (even if they were not implemented) | • These are a gold mine of wonderful ideas of all the dream items that hardly a system owner ever is allowed to implement due to conservative leaders in quality.
• It's excellent to revisit these because most times, it's more likely the ideas are too modern. And for a system like Agile-QMS, if it's too modern it's impossible for the antiquated software. So, if you're looking to modernize the QMS, it's likely staff have already come up with the idea and that it's recorded somewhere. (because companies are always trying to change the QMS). | • Going back to past workshops from previous, postponed, or outright cancelled projects saved us all a lot of work in not having to regenerate any work.
• A really good example of this is that while we were still very early in our relationship between the Parent company (Gilead) and the child company (Kite), we (Kite) had already led Design Thinking workshops to process map the shit out of what we fully wanted our QMS to be. So, I used those maps heavily to reconfirm with the Kite User Population that this was still valid and viable. It was. Saved me about 100 days of work to be honest with you and at the project start Kite was already leading the way in demonstrating what we wanted, and why we wanted it. |

Remember, keep these details to yourself unless they are actually needed (but have the details in a polished format ready to present if ever needed). They're for your historical perspective as the Project Manager or Business Lead. I like to say, keep this in your back pocket and pull it out only when necessary. The only exception is to allow these facts to be presented to the team you're trying to onboard and to your supervisor. Your supervisor, who will be helping through the political nightmare of a company with fledgling maturity, will need these details in his back pocket to manage them with his peers.

I know it may seem like an excessive amount of work, but if you know all of the above details, it will save you endless escalation type meetings like the one I highlighted where some doomsdayers wanted to remain in the status quo. Hitting them with facts about the finances was a very professional and polite way to steering them towards being an enterprise and global participant. And that leader actually thanked me for helping them see the bigger picture.

Regarding the collection of data, the evaluation of data, leading to data insights...

If you don't pay attention to anything else in this volume, then pay attention to this section and it may save your job if something goes horribly wrong when the system is finally implemented. The collection of the right kind of data is critical for data insights lending itself to Leaders actually finding you to be a credible Business Lead and Project Lead when you have factual answers to both their emotional and rational questions. With projects like these, most of the questions have an emotional origin through some subordinate who because they do not have the correct details freak out and escalate falsities. Eventually, I'll provide an example or two of false escalation but for now I intend to pivot to what data should be collected, what it looks like, and then let that bleed into the decision-making model.

Collecting the data, evaluating it, and turning the insights into marketing materials is the most critical and fundamental aspect to leading the implementation of the computerized QMS successfully, on-time, under budget, and right first time. I know! That's a bold statement. It's a "Mike Thing" and it has always served me well. Here's why: When you have a full understanding of what the data tells you then there is no question you cannot answer (both emotionally charged, or well thought out). And data insights are powerful allowing you to remain calm under fire because as I like to say, "the data is dynamic but also the data is the data – it cannot be debated". And, if you turn all of the data into beautiful marketing materials, then you will always have it at your fingertips when an emotional leader is trying to put you on the spot in a leadership type governance forum. I don't know about your experiences, but my last experience taught me to **always be presentation ready**. I found that I was in a leadership presentation at least five times per day and five days in a row. Because we were a global organization, there was one day I had to present to Amsterdam at 0200 PST. Six hours later (0800 PST) I was presenting to HQ. Three hours later (1100 PST), I was presenting to CA-TCF. One hour later (Noon PST) I was presenting to MD-TCF. It was both exhausting and exhilarating!

So, Mike, what data am I collecting, evaluating, and creating insights for? I created a table for the discussion. That said, the data that you must collect (and think of this as a module-by-module brainstorming activity):

1. Number of Users by Role per QMS Module – I call this the "User Community".
2. Will the to-be system have any new roles?
3. Record volume by type, category, or classification depending on the QMS module
4. What decisions need to be made regarding data migration?
5. How many controlled documents govern the QMS module and what are they?

6. Regarding the document control strategy, what will be required prior to go-live, at go-live, and post go-live?
7. What other QMS systems do the records connect to? (example: Deviation to CAPA)
8. What else needs to be considered? (Example: Reports, Dashboards, generation of metrics)
9. What's in it for the User?

Now that you know what you need to evaluate, let's discuss the why. I provide a template for the marketing materials below the table. For the sake of the below table let's use the example of the QMS Deviation module.

Data to Collect	Why?	Leading to these data insights…
User Community numbers by QMS module role	• This is the intended population to exist in the same roles in the corresponding new QMS module. • If they have the role now, it is likely they'll need the role when the new system is live.	• For example, there were 480 Deviation Owners and 180 Quality Approvers. • This is a very large population and now that we know those numbers we begin to think of what the training strategy will be. In my example, it was the middle of the year and we still did not know what the training strategy was going to be and that's just foreshadowing for an event that was escalated.
Now that you know the User Community by QMS module role, now dive deeper and assess how many records per person by classification there were	• This is a form of Pareto analysis helping the Project Lead understand exactly where all of the effort is being applied.	• What we learned was that only 20% of the Users who had access were actually active in the QMS Deviation module. • This is a significant data insight because it had us questioning whether or not the other 80% actually needed the access. Which also had us take a deep breath when thinking about the training strategy. Thoughts like, "Perhaps I don't have to train 500 people on a new system after all".
A new QMS typically has new roles compared to the previous QMS – Understand the new role and then collect data on	• If the new role does not have any Users in it at go-live, then the whole of the business will be shut down. •	• Records will be "stuck". Products will not be able to be dispositioned. The company will lose money.

what users will fill the role		
Record volume by type and/or classification, by site, and by functional area, and if you have enough bandwidth then also by Owner and Quality Approver	• Eventually, this will be critical towards the data migration effort. Knowing the volume helps the Project Lead understand eventually the amount of data that will be required to migrate to the new system. • Knowing the record volume by classification, type, by Owner, by Quality, by Site are all indicators of what to plan for relative to the customers and relative to what's in it for those customers. • Also, knowing this may lead to understanding business differences between business models across different sites.	• In the timeframe of interest, 7500 deviations were initiated. • 3900 (>50%) were minor. • 2300 were major. • 1100 were critical. • The most deviations were initiated at CA-TCF. Followed by AMSTERDAM-TCF. HQ hardly had any deviations. • There is a major difference in the process flow between CLINICAL-TCF and COMMERCIAL-TCF that will need to be considered in the process exercises.
How QMS records connect to other QMS records.	• Controlled program documents may need to also be revised depending on if they are system agnostic or not. • It's really important to understand the connectivity between the modules to ensure that the connectivity remains when the new system is implemented. • Also, there may be discovery of records in the current system that were previously unknown to you. Therefore, a strategy will need to be evaluated on what should occur given that situation.	• Example: LIR>DEV>CAPA>EV>CC>EV I flesh this out in great detail in the marketing materials below. • We learned that as Agile had been versioned there were different versions of Deviation, LIR, and Change Control Records. In fact, there were some deviations still open from the very first version of deviation and we were on version three. Also, BPDR records had versioned. • This led us to devising different data migration strategies for Deviation, LIR, Change Control, and BPDR records. That detail is provided in the Data Migration section.

Now that you know what data to collect and what data insights it can provide, the next step is to flesh out the marketing materials. The marketing materials below serve as a template for each QMS module that is intended to be implemented. In my case, our Phase 2 to implement the QMS intended to implement all of the "heavy hitters" as I like to say. Those being, Laboratory Investigation Reports (LIR), Deviations, Corrective Action Preventive Action (CAPA), Effectiveness Verification (EV), Change Control (CC), Product Complaints (PC), and Issue Escalation (IE). Note that these marketing materials will also eventually serve as presentations that will be provided to the leadership as well as onboarding the team. This is a critical point to make so that you're not constantly drafting materials and you are doing what you're supposed to be doing which is leading the project. I know it takes time. Your rushed self will thank you for this later though, I promise!

Marketing Materials using the Deviation Module as the example…

Deviation Module Deep Dive Preparation Leading up to Go-Live

User Community Insights:
- 20% of the Qualified User Community is active in Agile-QMS over the past 12 months.
- There are 500 Deviation Owners
- There are 185 Quality Approvers
- Assumption: All 685 users will access and therefore transition to the new QMS Deviation module.

New Role – Functional Area Approver – What do we know today?
- The role will be optional for Major/Critical deviations.
- The role will be optional because after reviewing the data for Major and Critical deviations, the majority of them ended up being for incoming material out of specifications which is a deviation type that cannot be corrected. The thought is that rigorous resources do not need to be applied.
- For all other Major/Critical deviations with root causes of Manpower, Machinery, Method, or Mother Nature, the FAA option must be exercised.
- The idea of the FAA is that this will be a centralized function limiting access to the experienced few.

What are CLINICAL-CA-TCF preferences?

Major/Critical Deviations by Root Cause Category

Category	Count
Method	1200
Manpower	900
Material	100
Mother Nature	100
Machinery	100

NOTE: Here, the Project Lead is already starting to consider any phase appropriate differences with the clinical manufacturing site. As it's part of the marketing materials, it's available for a conversation when clinical manufacturing is in attendance so that the Project Lead can begin gathering specific clinical-phase-appropriate quality management system differences.

Deviation Module Deep Dive Preparation Leading up to Go-Live

FAA Option 1	FAA Option 2	FAA Option 3
Centralize the FA Approver per department	**All Current Managers of existing User Community to have FA Approver Access**	**Hybrid of Options 1 & 2 at the discretion of the Site Leadership Team (SLT)**
• The idea is that there is one primary FA Approver per department. • This person is like a Head of their area or they are the primary delegate for the department. • They tend to have the most experience, are responsible for scheduling, usually a manager of managers.	• ~300 Managers would require training for FA Approver role. • Based on data insights of the existing user community, although these staff would be trained and have access it feels like they would hardly ever use the role.	To be socialized
• This option means there are very few FA Approvers which means although a new role, it is limited and requires little training. • This means the "right" approvers are approving Major/Critical deviations when the option is required or exercised to do so. • **GPO Recommendation Based on Data Insights: 1 primary FAA and one backup delegate FAA per department.**	• This is a decentralized model and is discouraged because the idea is an oversight and accountability model per ICHQ10.	To be socialized

The company will need to decide who / which option is best all data and all things considered

---

Deviation Module Deep Dive Preparation Leading up to Go-Live

New Role: Deviation Initiator

- Deviation Initiators start deviations when first observed and then later transfer to an Owner.
- This role has been requested by the business, namely manufacturing, to gain efficiencies in day-to-day processing of deviation records especially during shift changes.
- In Agile, one must go through comprehensive training to gain access as an Owner because Initiator is not a role in Agile and the role cannot be implemented in Agile due to it being antiquated.
- In Veeva, the Initiator will require less training because the role only allows the record to be progressed to classification. At classification, the record must be transferred to an Owner.
- There were ~7400 deviations initiated 01JAN2021-31MAY2022.
    - **~3900 Minor (which is where this role adds the greatest value proposition)**
    - ~2300 Major
    - ~1100 Critical

The company (each site) will need a decision on who will be an initiator.

Deviation Module Deep Dive Preparation Leading up to Go-Live

Demonstrating How Deviation Connects to other QMS Modules
- The below chevron map depicts parent child associations while coexisting in two QMSs.

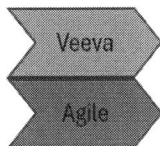

LIR → DEV → CAPA → EV → CC → EV

DEV → SCAR

Audit → CAPA

DEV → MRB

Veeva

Agile

! There are three examples where the company will have to be tolerant of existing in two QMSs.

? Do the Global Owners know and will those system SOPs require revision?

Deviation Module Deep Dive Preparation Leading up to Go-Live

Document Strategy Implementation Planning
- Controlled documents for deviation will have to consider coexisting in two QMSs.
- FACT: The current program documents are system specific to Agile-QMS.
- FACT: The Agile-QMS Deviation Module will be decommissioned 90 days after going live with Veeva.
- FACT: Parent-company will implement system agnostic controlled documents will be effective on go-live.
- FACT: Child-company has immunotherapy specific requirements and will maintain global documents.
- FACT: New Parent & Child Global Training Curricula will be required (obsolete the old).

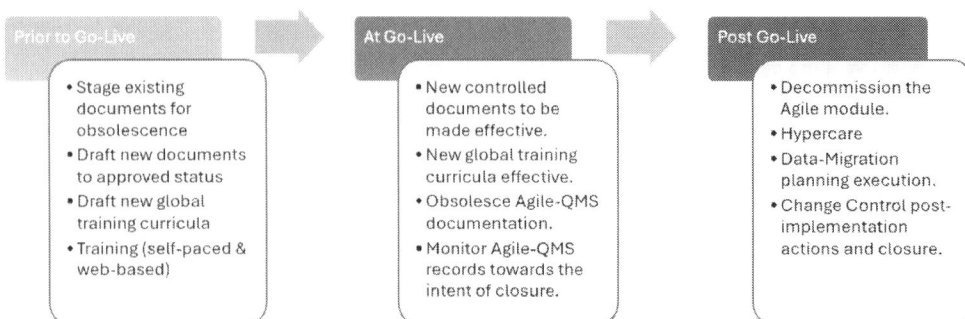

Prior to Go-Live
- Stage existing documents for obsolescence
- Draft new documents to approved status
- Draft new global training curricula
- Training (self-paced & web-based)

At Go-Live
- New controlled documents to be made effective.
- New global training curricula effective.
- Obsolesce Agile-QMS documentation.
- Monitor Agile-QMS records towards the intent of closure.

Post Go-Live
- Decommission the Agile module.
- Hypercare
- Data-Migration planning execution.
- Change Control post-implementation actions and closure.

Deviation Module Deep Dive Preparation Leading up to Go-Live

What else does Deviation require?

- Validated reports on record and object statuses
- Dashboards representative of quality management review statuses
- Quick Reference guides on reports and queries to generate lists for inspections (Inspectors).
- Dashboards representative of manufacturing work center teams (nice to have).
- **REQUIRED:** Disposition Report (Report generated to determine status of product impact assessments)
- **REQUIRED: Disposition Report – Final Product Disposition**

Marketing Materials using the CAPA Module as the example…

CAPA/EV Module Deep Dive Preparation Leading up to Go-Live

CAPA	Effectiveness Verification (EV)
450 CAPA Owners	600 EV Owners (the delta is that the access is shared with CC)
150 Quality Approvers	300 Quality Approvers

- Veeva is an object based platform. This means it has a parent record with objects associated to it.
- The parent record is known as a Quality Event (QE).
- So, each parent record starts off with QE, then a dash, then a number and the meta-data is what sets is apart as a stand alone record.
- Example: QE-0001 and the QMS Record = deviation.
- This is fundamentally different than Agile-QMS.
- In Agile-QMS each record is quality event.
- This is critical to highlight right now because EVs are parent records in Agile-QMS.
- EVs will be objects associated to a parent in Veeva.
- In Agile-QMS, EV access is obtained when you are trained on CAPA or Change Control or both.
- In Veeva-QMS, EV access is provided when you are trained on CAPA or Change Control.
- In Veeva-QMS, EV is one object that can be associated to any Parent Record. It cannot be a stand alone record (like we have right now).

• 100 CAPAs per quarter	• 30 EVs per quarter
• Only 20% of the population is active.	• Only 10% of the population is active

CAPA/EV Module Deep Dive Preparation Leading up to Go-Live

Sources of CAPA and Effectiveness Verification	
CAPA	**Effectiveness Verification (EV)**
17 Sources	5 Sources
Examples... • Annual Product Review • BPDR • Internal Audit • Gap Assessment • Document Control Revision Gap Assessment • Deviation • Root Cause Analysis • Product Complaint • Quality Management Review • Change Control • Risk Management	Examples... • CAPA • Change Control • Deviation • SCAR • Risk Management

The controlled documents associated to these sources will be evaluated to determine if they should be revised

CAPA/EV Module Deep Dive Preparation Leading up to Go-Live

FAA Option 1	FAA Option 2
• The idea is that there is one primary FA Approver per department. • This person is like a Head of their area or they are the primary delegate for the department. • They tend to have the most experience, are responsible for scheduling, usually a manager of managers.	• ~300 Managers would require training for FA Approver role. • Based on data insights of the existing user community, although these staff would be trained and have access it feels like they would hardly ever use the role.
• This option means there are very few FA Approvers which means although a new role, it is limited and requires little training. • **GPO Recommendation Based on Data Insights: 1 primary FAA and one backup delegate FAA per department.**	• This is a decentralized model and is discouraged because the idea is an oversight and accountability model per ICHQ10.

The company will need to decide who / which option is best all data and all things considered

CAPA/EV Module Deep Dive Preparation Leading up to Go-Live

Document Strategy Implementation Planning

- Controlled documents for CAPA/EV will have to consider coexisting in two QMSs.
- FACT: The current program documents are system specific to Agile-QMS.
- FACT: The Agile-QMS CAPA/EV Module will be decommissioned 90 days after going live with Veeva.
- FACT: Parent-company will implement system agnostic controlled documents effective on go-live.
- FACT: Child-company has immunotherapy specific requirements and will maintain global documents.
- FACT: New Parent & Child Global Training Curricula will be required (obsolete the old).

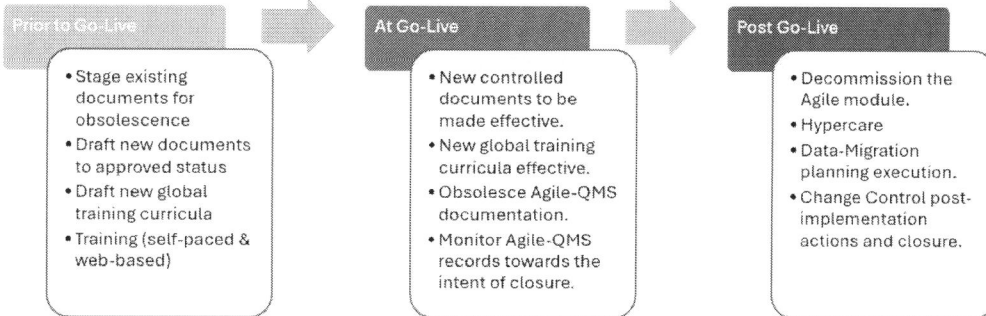

Prior to Go-Live	At Go-Live	Post Go-Live
• Stage existing documents for obsolescence • Draft new documents to approved status • Draft new global training curricula • Training (self-paced & web-based)	• New controlled documents to be made effective. • New global training curricula effective. • Obsolesce Agile-QMS documentation. • Monitor Agile-QMS records towards the intent of closure.	• Decommission the Agile module. • Hypercare • Data-Migration planning execution. • Change Control post-implementation actions and closure.

Marketing Materials using the Change Control Module as the example...

Change Control Module Deep Dive Preparation Leading up to Go-Live

Change Control
400 Change Control Owners
200 Quality Approvers
500 Impact Assessors with 20 of them in Regulatory Affairs

- The company is growing – The number of change control is increasing as the company licenses more products and joins other jurisdictions.

Change Control Module Deep Dive Preparation Leading up to Go-Live

NEW: Initiator Role	Change Owner	NEW: FA Approver	Quality Approver
• New capability in the QMS with a Change Proposal Process. • Only Change Initiators will have the access to initiate a change proposal.	• Same as Agile-QMS.	• Required for all changes regardless of risk classification and regardless of the change being global or not global.	• Same as Agile-QMS.

FAA Option 1	FAA Option 2
• The idea is that there is one primary FA Approver per department. • This person is like a Head of their area or they are the primary delegate for the department. • They tend to have the most experience, are responsible for scheduling, usually a manager of managers.	• ~300 Managers would require training for FA Approver role.
• This option means there are very few FA Approvers which means although a new role, it is limited and requires little training. • **GPO Recommendation Based on Data Insights: 1 primary FAA and one backup delegate FAA per department.**	• This is a decentralized model and is discouraged because the idea is an oversight and accountability model per ICHQ10.

Change Control Module Deep Dive Preparation Leading up to Go-Live

Demonstrating How Change Control Connects to other QMS Modules
- The below chevron map depicts parent child associations while coexisting in two QMSs.

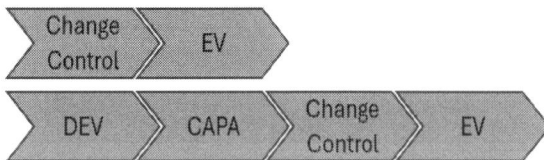

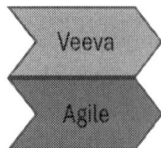

Change Control → EV

DEV → CAPA → Change Control → EV

Veeva

Agile

- In the change space, all will be in one QMS.
- ? Do the Global Owners know and will those system SOPs require revision?

Change Control Module Deep Dive Preparation Leading up to Go-Live

Document Strategy Implementation Planning

- Controlled documents for CC will have to consider coexisting in two QMSs.
- FACT: The current program documents are system specific to Agile-QMS.
- FACT: The Agile-QMS CC Module will be decommissioned 90 days after going live with Veeva.
- FACT: Parent-company will implement system agnostic controlled documents effective on go-live.
- FACT: Child-company has immunotherapy specific requirements and will maintain global documents.
- FACT: New Parent & Child Global Training Curricula will be required (obsolete the old).

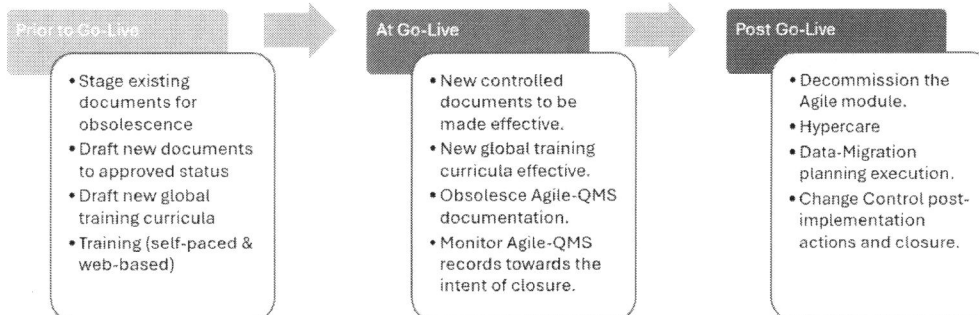

Prior to Go-Live
- Stage existing documents for obsolescence
- Draft new documents to approved status
- Draft new global training curricula
- Training (self-paced & web-based)

At Go-Live
- New controlled documents to be made effective.
- New global training curricula effective.
- Obsolesce Agile-QMS documentation.
- Monitor Agile-QMS records towards the intent of closure.

Post Go-Live
- Decommission the Agile module.
- Hypercare
- Data-Migration planning execution.
- Change Control post-implementation actions and closure.

Of course, that's not even close to being the end of the marketing materials. The materials need to have an agenda, the team defined, roles and responsibilities, scope, high-level timeline, zoomed-in timeline (8-week view), project dashboard with status, and so on and so forth. These are forthcoming in future chapters.

Remember, all this hard but excellent work is to keep you grounded in reality on what your current state is. If you do not know your current state, then you cannot get to a future state. Well, I mean, you can, but it will be disorganized, fraught with escalation, and will most likely be implemented wrong first time!

Decision Making Model

For companies that do not have a decision-making model there are only two other options available; an escalation model or a consensus building model. In the eight firms I've been a full-time employee of, only two had a decision-making model. Then, the least mature organizations had an escalation model. The more mature had a consensus building model. Trust me when I tell you that the escalation model is a horrible experience and one I hope to never experience again. It's contemptuous and costly because the escalated topic tends to circle up to corporate leadership, circle back down to site leadership, then to site owners, and then is revisited numerous times with all of the staff in between and no one ever really knows where it landed. In other words, it will linger and if it lingers for too long it may actually impact the schedule and the timing of going-live.

Consensus building is great. Except when you have to obtain consensus from over 5000 staff who are in different niches of the organization such as medical device, biologics, GCP, small molecule and immunotherapy. All of that said, everyone has worthy intent, and they all believe they are "right" for the greater cause. And they are not wrong. So, if a company does not subscribe to a decision-making model, then the project and actually being able to implement the computerized QMS is doomed from the start. Because, no one understands or knows who is in charge. And staff in this space have a lot of onus and accountability so they wonder…Is it me!?? (and then they react accordingly!)

Great, so what if you do have a decision-making model but no one knows about it and it's not accepted nor widely used. At one of the last places I worked there was an amazing decision-making model. One of the best I've ever seen. That said, hardly anyone was trained on it, hardly anyone knew about it, so it was never used. I once disguised a QMS improvement presentation to the Head of Quality and Head of QC in a decision-making format. It was brilliant. It had context. It had stakeholder advice ready for review, and then the end was the two Heads to render their decision considering all of the options and advice.

And in one short hour, we had two top cheeses rendering a decision. The folks in the meeting who were not in charge but had a vested interest, were side messaging me like crazy. "Wow! This has never happened before. What! Are you some kind of wizard!". I hope you're laughing. I'm just trying to convey that a decision-making model is powerful when used correctly but more importantly when everyone understands that this is the standard. So, upfront in the project, leadership must agree to the model and then the Project Lead and Business Lead must use the model effectively and consistently. Additionally, the model must be overly socialized in all forums to all informed stakeholders otherwise people, as a natural tendency think it's their remit or their supervisor's remit and then bring back the escalation and consensus models.

The model below (Figure 1) is one I've subscribed to several times to implement a computerized QMS. It's simple, straightforward, and hints at the team's roles and responsibilities. And like I said, if socialized and everyone adopts it, then it leads to vast amounts of professionalism and courtesy. It also leads to landing all project milestones on time.

The figure is set up with the timing component to the left, the order of staff responsible for a decision, and then the decision in their remit. It's critical during the onboarding of the team that you highlight for staff where exactly they fit into the decision-making model. For example, at Kite, we had a corporate staff known as Global Program Owners who fit into the Project Core Team and the Focused Team. Then we had Site Process Owners at each of the manufacturing sites who mostly fit into the Sites and QMS Users. This was controversial for them because they felt they would have more decision-making influence. As Project Lead, I loved their passion because we definitely needed a lot of their support since they were actually in the trenches doing the work and I vied for them (to my detriment) to be in the Extended Team.

One final note. Although this is a decision-making model, you can also see firsthand that this is the pathway for escalation as well. That's the beauty of it. And, this model should always be present in any and all meetings regarding the project. In my case it was Champion's meetings (more on that later), weekly network (all networks) meetings, Kite-specific Core Team Meetings, Kite-specific extended team meetings, Site Leadership Team meetings, Global Leadership Team meetings, and etc – the meetings are endless which is to be expected. Anyway, give this a review and see what you can take away from it for your project and hopefully your benefit.

Figure 1 – Project Decision Making Model

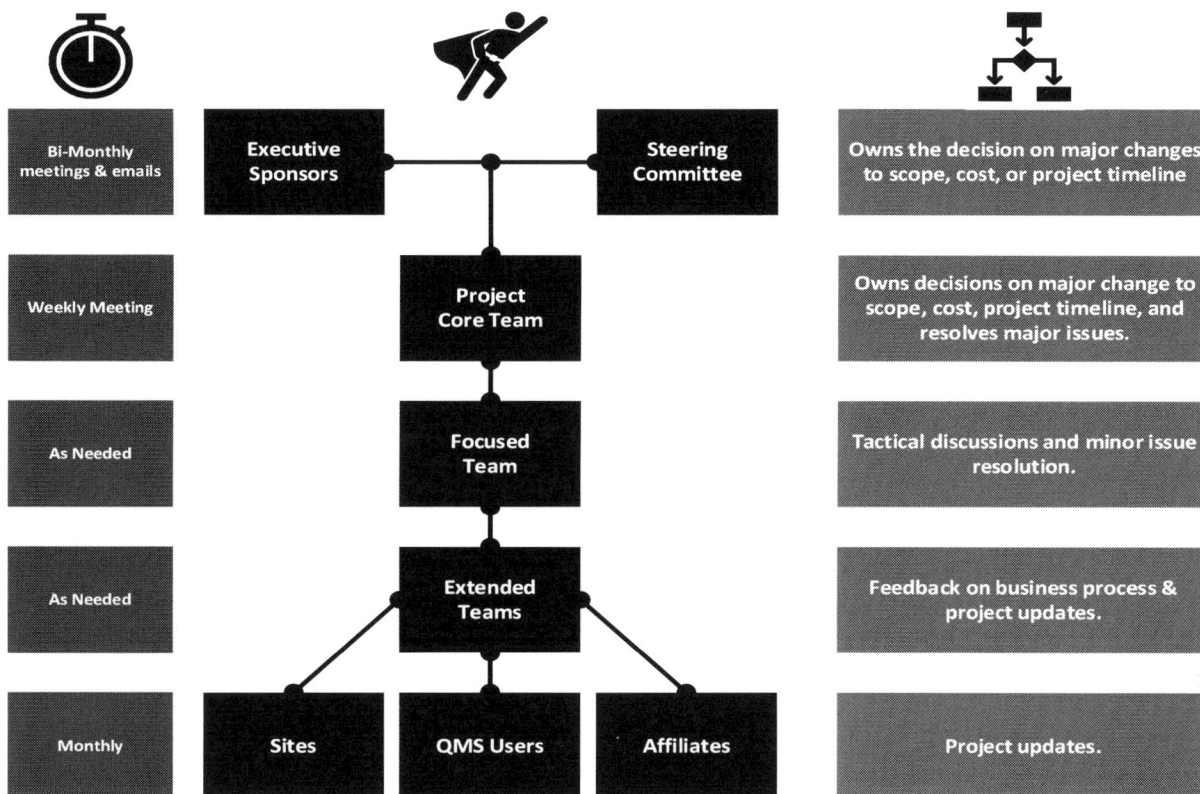

		Owns the decision on major changes to scope, cost, or project timeline
Bi-Monthly meetings & emails	Executive Sponsors / Steering Committee	
Weekly Meeting	Project Core Team	Owns decisions on major change to scope, cost, project timeline, and resolves major issues.
As Needed	Focused Team	Tactical discussions and minor issue resolution.
As Needed	Extended Teams	Feedback on business process & project updates.
Monthly	Sites / QMS Users / Affiliates	Project updates.

Defining roles and responsibilities…

Estimated Time Commitment

Focused Team Time Estimate
- Anticipate 25% of time per module (10 hours / week) for the entirety of the project.

Extended Team Time Estimate
- Anticipate 10-20% of time per module (4-8 hours / week) for the entirety of the project.

● ● ● **Other Considerations**
  - We generally know **only** 6-8 weeks out what major activities we'll be participating in.
  - Most of us are in zoom – we are attempting to be more face to face.
  - Travel must be approved by VP of Quality.
  - We know this is not your day-job and that you'll have Site work in parallel.
  - Designate an appropriate back up when appropriate given your priorities – onboard them!

Project Business Leads & Focused Leads

- 100% dedicated.
- Responsible for leading the implementation roll-out at sites across all in scope modules per defined and approved phases.
- Serve as the single point of contact and change agent for their defined entity.
- Identify and recruit extended leads.
- Track revisions to controlled documents from their entity.
- Establish entity specific user requirements with justifications for user requirements that are additional or in conflict with Parent company requirements.
- ID user community and prepare community for Parent company training expectations.
- Communicate updates per communication plan.
- Communicate with entity leadership towards the end of resource allocation and support.
- Responsible for successful change adoption through expositions and roadshows.

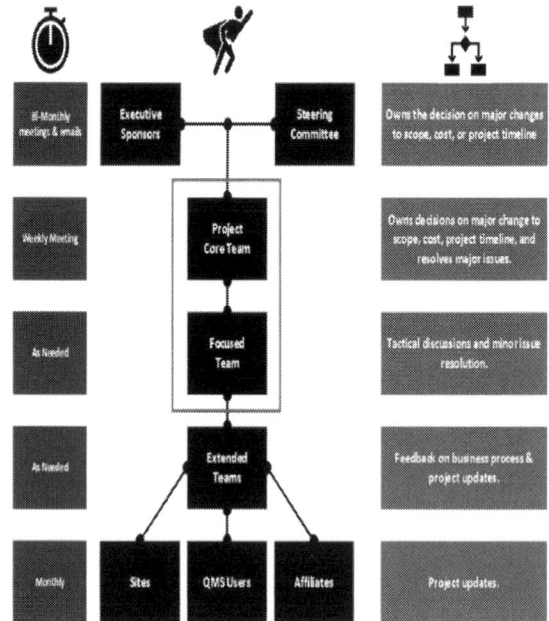

Focused Lead Global Program Owner Responsibilities

Focused Lead GPO Responsibilities

- Responsible for the implementation of the module.
- Drives alignment of the business process with site process owners with an enterprise mindset first and always.
- Supports effective meetings; deescalates conflict.
- The decision maker for the module.
- Leads communication efforts at the site level specifically with site leadership and all module stakeholders.
- Partners with Organization Change Management to ensure communicates are right given known business preferences.
- Partners with computerized system team to address configuration challenges.
- Assists with training development.

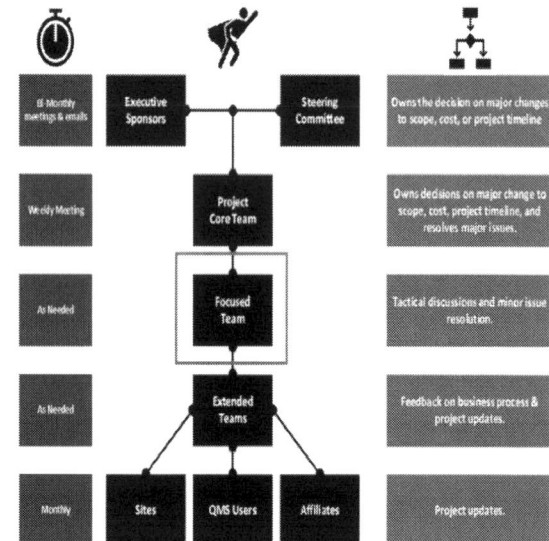

Figure 1 – Project Decision Making Model

Focused Lead Responsibilities

- Supports modules of responsibility and evangelizes the to-be system to the sites for adoption.
- Supports decisions for the enterprise, the site, and the function.
- When delegating work, ensure a thorough onboarding plan to minimize business disruption.

- Actively participate in workshops to provide business preferences and practices, context, verify controlled documents, and complete all workshop pre-work and actual work.
- Provide centralized and aggregate feedback on solutions during each process exercise phase based on process exercise scope.
- Provide centralized and aggregate feedback on functional use cases, operational challenges, and the user experience.
- Identify risks and propose mitigation actions.

- Work with the extended team during reviews and assessments to help gather feedback in the scope of the process exercise.
- Act as a change agent to communicate decisions of the project team to sites and functional areas.
- Collect and provide feedback on controlled documents including procedures and training.
- Participate as a subject matter expert in the system during testing and process exercises.
- Support the development of user community training.

Extended Team Responsibilities

Extended Team Responsibilities

- Coordinates with the Focus Team Lead for their site or functional area.
- Participates in Process Exercise hands on testing.
- Collects and provides feedback to the Focus Team Representative on the solution at each system iteration including any stakeholder needs based on business use cases.
- Acts as change agent for their organization, site, or functional area.
- Assigns back up and onboards them if/when they're going to be out of the office.

Figure 1 – Project Decision Making Model

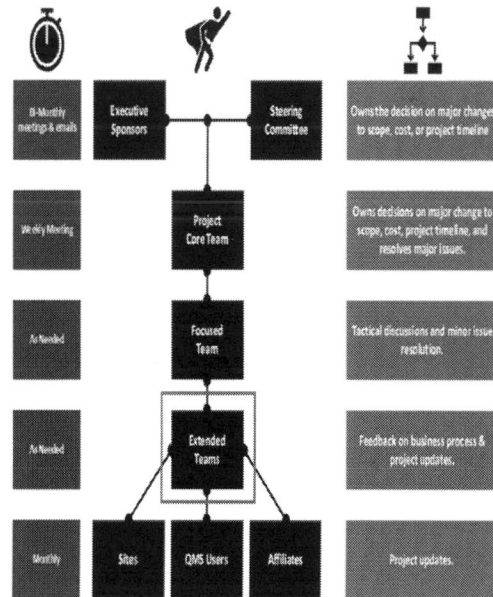

Chapter 5
The Veeva Timeline and the Phased Approach that can be used for all eQMSs

In leading the implementation of Veeva as a Project Lead for Kite on behalf of Gilead it was no small feat and it was the most challenging and the most rewarding activity of my 30-year career. The way this project unfolds is in phases. Below is an example of how the phased approach is designed for the massive task of implementing a new, enterprise computerized quality management system. Note that this diagram represents one phase. Yes, each phase requires 1-year of dedicated effort by all of those listed above has having a role or a responsibility using the below format.

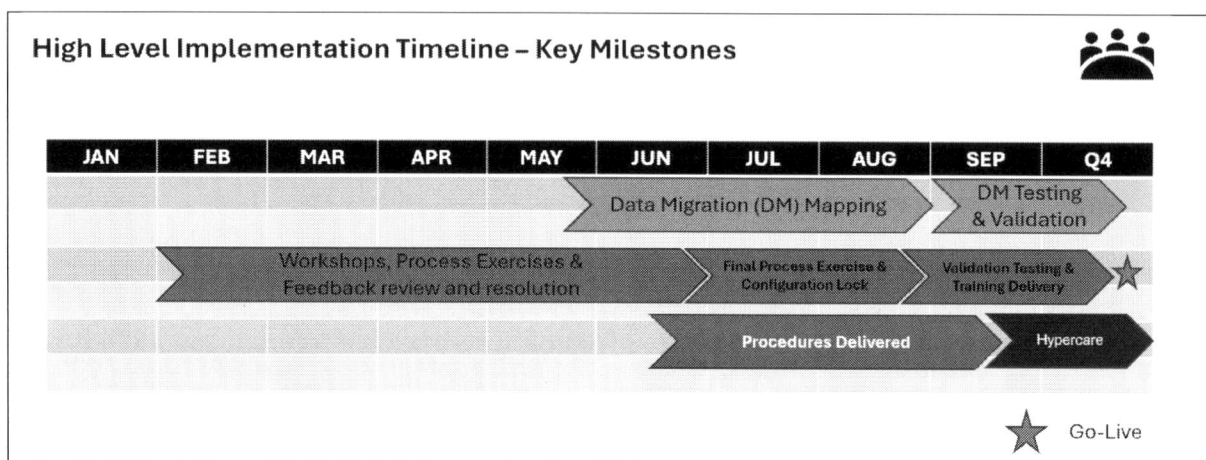

High Level Implementation Timeline – Key Milestones

JAN	FEB	MAR	APR	MAY	JUN	JUL	AUG	SEP	Q4

Data Migration (DM) Mapping

DM Testing & Validation

Workshops, Process Exercises & Feedback review and resolution

Final Process Exercise & Configuration Lock

Validation Testing & Training Delivery

Procedures Delivered

Hypercare

Go-Live

We implemented Veeva in three phases with specific modules by phase and it looked something like this:

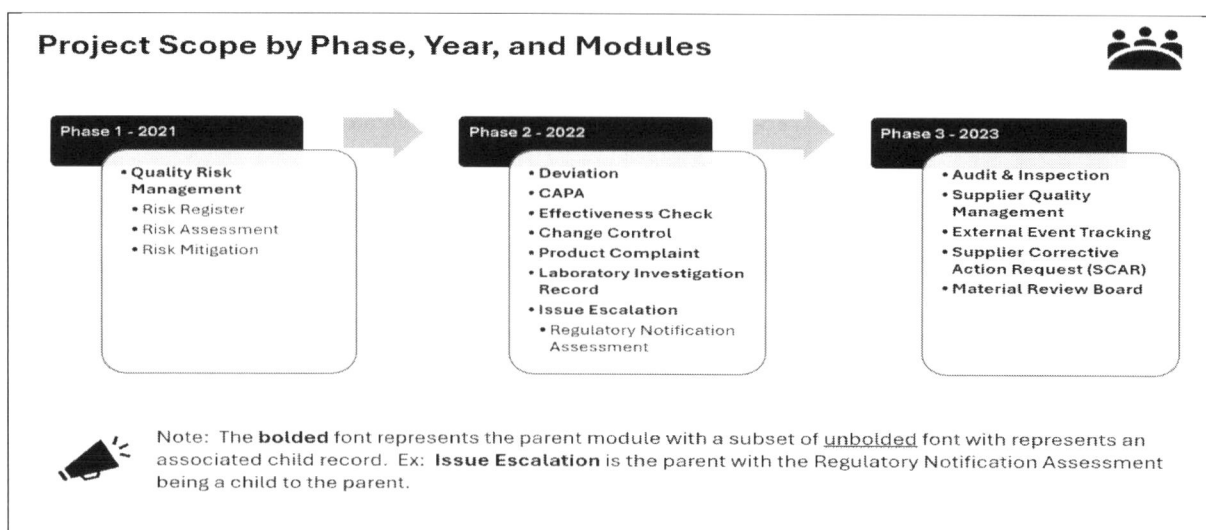

Project Scope by Phase, Year, and Modules

Phase 1 - 2021
- **Quality Risk Management**
  - Risk Register
  - Risk Assessment
  - Risk Mitigation

Phase 2 - 2022
- **Deviation**
- **CAPA**
- **Effectiveness Check**
- **Change Control**
- **Product Complaint**
- **Laboratory Investigation Record**
- **Issue Escalation**
  - Regulatory Notification Assessment

Phase 3 - 2023
- **Audit & Inspection**
- **Supplier Quality Management**
- **External Event Tracking**
- **Supplier Corrective Action Request (SCAR)**
- **Material Review Board**

Note: The **bolded** font represents the parent module with a subset of unbolded font with represents an associated child record. Ex: **Issue Escalation** is the parent with the Regulatory Notification Assessment being a child to the parent.

The above diagram represents a nearly ideal way of implementing these modules. I'll attempt to wax poetic as to the reasons why as well as offer one anecdote about how we could have implemented this even better than how we did relative to the order of the modules.

First, one must understand that Veeva is segmented. I'm sure there's a technical term for what I mean and it's the only word I could come up with. Think of Quality Risk Management (QRM) as its own segment. This segment is separated from all of the other Veeva segments. Contained within the QRM segment are the records you see unbolded and indented to the bolded. QRM is the segment and contained in the segment is the Risk Register (RR), the Risk Assessment (RA), and the Risk Mitigation (RM). As such, this is how they are enumerated within the module of QRM. RR-00001, equals the first risk register in the QRM module. I think you understand what I mean.

Why is this important? This is important because Veeva likes to take credit for how extraordinary their system is relative to querying and reportability. They claim to have google-like search capability. This is true, but at the time of this writing, the google-like search capability can only be executed in the segment that the person is using. In other words, you cannot google-like search across the segments. If you complete a search in the QRM module, the search is contained to the QRM module. That said, there is a way to marry the objects in the reporting module so that you are still able to query and report across the modules. And that is very significant and truly a remarkable feature of Veeva.

Phase 2 of the project had the "heavy hitter" quality system modules as I like to say. The majority of those are called Quality Events (QE) and within quality events are Quality Actions (QA). This is important to note because the search capability is contained in QEs if that's where you performed the search and does not cross over into the QAs. Deviations, for example are a Quality Event. The Deviation record itself is a Parent Object. And associated to a Deviation are objects such as a Product Impact Assessment (PIA). The PIA is a Quality Action (QA). Therefore, a google-like search may not be appropriate when attempting to query for some product lot number because one would have to consider the search in both the QE segment and the QA segment. This is where reporting is critical because a QE-Deviation can be married to a QA-PIA of that deviation so that the product impact can be queried, let's say, for a lot disposition report as one critical example for all pharma companies.

In any case, implementing the modules in this manner really makes the most logical sense. Phase 1 implemented QRM. Most companies do not consider QRM to be a quality system and therefore do not place it into their quality management system. It's best to start with QRM because the Risk Managers are using noncompliant ways or work arounds for managing risk. Usually, Risk Management is completed in SmartSheets, OneNote, or the Universe forbid, Microsoft Access or Excel. These programs are not validated therefore it's not compliant to manage it this way. Also, Knowledge Management of Risk, and Risk Assessment is nearly impossible with these methods and the reality is, if you don't have visibility to your risks, you run the risk of stocking out. Anyway, this way of managing risk is really absurd because all computerized QMSs have an out of the box configuration for Risk Management.

Regarding the work around. Sometimes the more sophisticated Risk Managers will manage risk assessments via Document Control. It's a smart workaround and it technically places Risk Management in a quality system that is validated. However, if that person leaves the company, they're usually the only one who knew where everything was and then some poor Document Control person has to make their best attempts to think like that person and find all of the possible documents that fit into the Risk Assessment space. Of course, not all of them are found or identified which leads to a slight risk to Inspection Readiness, and well, managing risks that were assessed and perhaps still might require mitigation.

Final thought on why to implement QRM first: In addition to that most companies do not have QRM in the QMS, I'd would just highlight that ICHQ10 requires Risk Management as part of the Pharmaceutical Quality Management System, and ICHQ9 provides the explicit infrastructure to make it so. In other words, it's required by law so start here as a strong foundation for the rest of the QMS. And remember to keep this module simple because simplicity breeds compliance.

This reminds me of a fun story where I was starting to realize that I might actually be a good quality leader. All best-in-class project management for projects, in addition to defining the roles and responsibilities must have a succession plan and must also have an onboarding packet to expeditiously bring any new team member up to speed. Refer to the previous chapters on the marketing materials!

My supervisor decided to take a new position near the end of Phase 1. In other words, close to the point in time we would be live with the Veeva-QRM module. I was named the interim Head of the QMS, the Kite Business & Project Lead to implement Veeva, and I was also asked to lead what we coined the BioNTech Transition. I was also handed a team who were the smartest team I've ever had yet they were the least experienced in all of my thirty years. I'll say it again: This was the most difficult charge of my career and also the most rewarding. As a Quality Leader, the first thing I realized was that I had to learn how to trust my team. At the same time, the Global Program Owner (GPO) for Risk was leaving the company and did not name a new GPO. And this is the most critical point in time to implement the QRM module. Are you panicking? Because writing those words makes my own heart rate rise! I'm not joking.

As the interim Head of the QMS, I met with the Head of Quality at HQ and together we named a new GPO of Risk. Once the announcement was made, I met with him to get a feel for what he knew was going on with Veeva-QRM implementation. To my surprise he knew nothing at all! Ever have that sinking feeling in your gut that something is about to go horribly wrong? Yes, that's how I was feeling. I assured the new GPO that everything was going to be okay and if he trusted me we were about to go on the Mike thing journey.

So, new GPO of Risk and myself meet in person. By the way this was at the height of the pandemic when there was not even a vaccine. So, we meet, masks on, hunker down, and really do the deep dive of any materials we can find from Gilead on how the system should work, the process exercises, the marketing materials, as well as a deep dive of the system itself.

The GPO is eerily quiet. I'm alarmed. So, I ask him with a little bit of bias, "Hey man, are you ok? This looks pretty good for the first ever of its kind Risk Register and QRM module. Your team did a great job here". "Well, actually Mike, I hate it. This is not good at all. You know how much work this is going to be for the Risk Managers at all of the sites. They're going to give us a lot of adverse feedback".

All of the blood drained from my face and I turned porcelain white. The GPO of Risk wanted to call all stop on the implementation of the QRM module twenty days before we were going to be live with it. He was young, but super smart and very experienced in the Risk Management space and as the Project Lead and as a Quality Leader I had to give him the benefit of the doubt and I had to take this seriously.

My experiences though, had not prepared me for this and I really did not know what to do. I looked at him seriously, and I said, "Are you sure, Mr. GPO? Because to me, what you're calling out is normal quality management system things. Like, this is normal". Mr. GPO's concern was that there were a lot of fields in the record to populate in order to call the record complete. His other concern was that there was a lot of manual processing within the Risk Assessment workflow. In total there were nearly 100 actions or tasks to manage per each Risk Assessment. Said differently, each row of a Risk Assessment was now a new task to manage and every task had its own lifecycle.

In the current process, each Risk Assessment was viewed comprehensively in one document and then uploaded to SmartSheet and Veeva-Document Control. In other words, the Risk Managers would have 100 tasks in the new process versus 1 task in the old. And if you remember from a previous chapter, the point of all of this was to give the User Community a simplified experience. This implementation was giving the User Community a more complex process and experience. Mr. GPO was right. The User Community was going to be very upset and the Risk Managers were known to be a very vocal group.

I realized in this moment, that to this point, it was just the two of us speaking so I formed a Kite sub-group of all of my Business Leads and we met in a hybrid in-person and zoom format. I let Mr. GPO articulate his concerns to this Business Lead subgroup and we actually reached consensus. To point one, this was all just normal QMS field entry so there was nothing to escalate to Gilead from that perspective. And to point two, everyone agreed that 1 task turning into 100 was not simple, perhaps out of compliance, and definitely not built as intended. So, we raised the red flag.

I thought we were going to get into trouble. In fact, I was taken off the project (even though I had just started and it was not my call for how we got here). Gilead ended up agreeing with us. We reconfigured the module and rescheduled the go-live date to 30 days beyond the original go-live date. In the end we were superheroes who were bold enough to come forward with a problem statement, and a working solution. Trust me, rescheduling a system implementation 30 days from the original go-live date is hardly an impact vs impacting an entire organization with a system that would have delayed the business as well as being super expensive. We estimated that each site (Gilead and Kite) would have needed three extra resources to manage Risk Tasks in Risk Assessments. That's $1 million dollars in extra head count per year!

By the way, I was able to use my marketing materials, which now contained this problem statement, the solution, and how much money it saved, with the Head of Quality, who immediately reinstated me as the Project Lead and Business Lead for Kite with the first ever of its kind apology. (Head's of Quality are full of themselves and rarely can admit if or when they are wrong!)

Anyway, in a company that already has Document Control and Training in Veeva, the first logical module to implement is Quality Risk Management. Do yourselves a favor and do not over-configure it. Take it out of the box. It's an excellent solution out of the box. Then, implement the heavy hitters. The heavy hitters go next because it's the heaviest lift. Since you went with a simple implementation in Phase 1, you've basically completed your practice run to take on the majority of the project implementation. You've gained the experience to make the next phase successful. Also, the modules in Phase 2 usually consist of the same population. So, you're less likely to impact the Enterprise's resources in terms of the duration of time needed. They will only participate in Phase 2 so it's best to complete those modules all at once.

Then, the Phase 3 modules are ancillary to the Phase 2 modules which is why it makes sense to implement them as the final phase of the project. Usually in parallel to implementing Change Control, Regulatory Affairs is implementing the Regulatory Information Management System (RIMS) which connects to Change Control. That's a very important side note for the Project Lead and Business Lead to make sure there is some connection there because for whatever reason that I cannot determine, these tend to be separate Veeva Projects with different Veeva Teams and different Parent company leadership. In other words they're separate projects even though they are closely related and in fact are connected.

The anecdote...

In the QRM module, what exactly is Risk Mitigation? I'll tell you what it is. It's a CAPA. So, instead of wasting any time and effort into creating a Risk Mitigation record, do yourselves a favor and just implement the Quality Event-CAPA record. I know, it's a radical idea but it's also super simple. And simplicity breeds compliance!

Final thought: At the most critical stage leading into go-live, the project leader and risk GPO left one after another, causing great uncertainty in the entire implementation process. This made me realize that succession planning and knowledge inheritance are crucial in corporate management. An excellent project should not only focus on the implementation of technology but also ensure the stability of the team and the continuation of experience, otherwise even the best system will be difficult to run successfully. So how do you do that, Mike? It's simple, you execute Process Exercises in Sprint format. Keep reading.

The Process Exercise Methodology Completed in Sprint Format

When implementing the computerized QMS, the Project Team must optimize the user experience and improve data interoperability between modules, functions, and thinking globally, the entirety of the organization. **This is achieved by Process Exercises completed in a Sprint format.**

This is considered best in class. One may debate me that this seems overly rigorous and is too expensive upfront. Well let me tell you a story about that. In a parallel project, implementing a disposition module, the project team did not use the best-in-class methodology. As a result, data did not migrate correctly on go-live. As such, the CEO of the company had to intervene, and the unfortunate outcome was that product could not be dispositioned. Put into business terms, the company lost profits for a period that year. Trust me, heads rolled. I still stand in shock to think that a CEO of one of the largest pharma companies on the planet had to become involved at the project level and call *all stop*. I know that you have to support your boss and that your boss thinks this is overly rigorous and costly. Tell them this story because not building quality into the front means deviations, defects, and rework on the back end. And it's more expensive to fix those on the back end versus the meager costs of quality up front. (this is precisely what this volume is actually about!)

Let's start with the basics.

What is a Process Exercise?

A Process Exercise is a set of instructions that follow a sequential order for a User to follow in so that they may process a record in a specific module from the beginning of the record to the end of the record. As such, a User will take on all of the roles of the record such as Owner, Functional Area Approver, and Quality Approver in order to move the record through its lifecycle.

The Process Exercise usually assumes the best-case scenario especially in the first two sprints. The Process Exercise instructions will be module specific. The Process Exercise instructions will define key aspects of the system, highlight key capabilities and will be designed as such that the User cannot break the system, the workflow, nor the record. Administrative members are available if something is confusing or difficult to understand. In short, a Process Exercise represents the configuration of the record and its workflow – how to process a record. Additionally, the Process Exercise is standardized across modules and serves as the consistent way to process a record for the purposes of feedback collection, evaluation of feedback, review, and reconfiguration of the record, workflow, or the system.

What is a Sprint?

A Sprint is a time-boxed period where a team focuses on completing the Process Exercises with the goal of delivering a working product by the end of the time frame.

Time-boxed:

- Each sprint has a fixed duration, meaning the team must complete their planned work within that time frame.

Iterative development:

- Sprints allow for continuous improvement and adaptation by delivering small, working pieces of software in each cycle.

Sprint planning:

- Before each sprint, the team holds a planning meeting to define the sprint goal, select tasks from the product backlog, and estimate the work involved.

Daily scrums:

- During a sprint, teams often have daily stand-up meetings ("daily scrums") to discuss progress, identify roadblocks, and adjust plans as needed.

Benefits of using sprints:

Faster feedback:

- Teams can get feedback from stakeholders frequently throughout the development process.

Increased flexibility:

- Ability to adapt to changing requirements more easily by adjusting work within each sprint.

Improved collaboration:

- Encourages team members to work together towards a common goal within each sprint.

Measurable progress:

- Each sprint delivers a tangible outcome, allowing for better project tracking and visibility.

What is the 4x4 Sprint format?

The 4x4 Sprint format is a short-hand method of representing that the Veeva sprint process exercise methodology will be completed with four sprints where each sprint lasts 4 weeks and each sprint has a pre-determined scope.

Each Sprint is executed conceptually in the following way relative to scope:

- Week 1 – Requirements Gathering
- Week 2 – Configuration
- Week 3 – Process Exercises
- Week 4 – Feedback Review and Reconfiguration

Each of the four sprints is designed to tackle a specific scope of the system such as:

- Sprint 1:
    - System Lifecycle
    - System Workflows
    - Data Fields
- Sprint 2:
    - Field Rules
    - Workflow Automation
    - Reports
- Sprint 3:
    - Security Logic

- o Roles / Permissions
- o Formatted Outputs
- Sprint 4:
  - o Reports & Dashboards

The Process Exercise Methodology

1. **Hands on Evaluation**
   1. The Process Exercise is based on a combination of the delivered application and enterprise-specific requirements.
2. **Feedback Gathered**
   1. Feedback is entered in the Process Exercise feedback recording tool (like a SmartSheet) and is reviewed by the Focused Team.
3. **Process Exercise Review**
   1. Daily office hours to support teams with questions/concerns/feedback/errors.
   2. Feedback is actively monitored with updates and status reviews to determine acceptance or justification for not implementing.
4. **Configuration Updates**
   1. The configuration team will configure all agreed upon changes or fixes.
   2. Changes are socialized through office hours and other daily communication mediums.

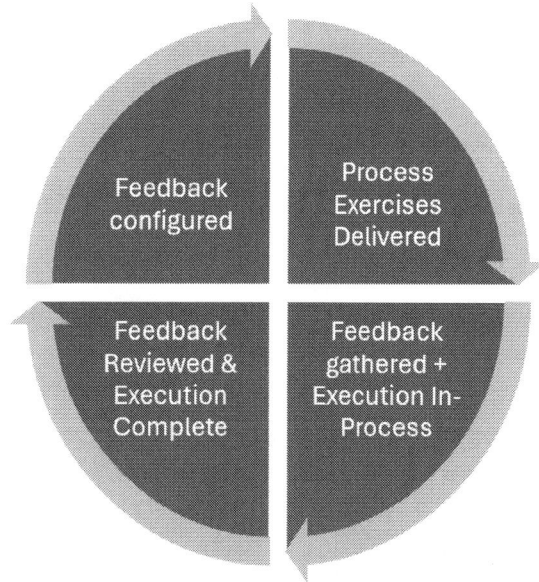

Feedback configured → Process Exercises Delivered → Feedback gathered + Execution In-Process → Feedback Reviewed & Execution Complete

---

The Sprint Format

- WEEK 1 – Requirements
- WEEK 2 – Configuration
- WEEK 3 – Process Exercises
- WEEK 4 – Feedback & Configuration

MON	TUE	WED	THU	FRI
Deviation CAPA	Change Control	Product Complaints	LIRs	Issue Escalation

The 4x4 Sprint Format

FEB2025						
S	M	T	W	T	F	S
	D/C	CC	PC	LIR	IE	1
2	3	4	5	6	7	8
9	10	11	12	13	14	15
16	17	18	19	20	21	22
23	24	25	26	27	28	

MAR2025						
S	M	T	W	T	F	S
	D/C	CC	PC	LIR	IE	1
2	3	4	5	6	7	8
9	10	11	12	13	14	15
16	17	18	19	20	21	22
23	24	25	26	27	28	29
30	31					

APR2025						
S	M	T	W	T	F	S
	D/C	CC	PC	LIR	IE	
		1	2	3	4	5
6	7	8	9	10	11	12
13	14	15	16	17	18	19
20	21	22	23	24	25	26
27	28	29	30			

MAY2025						
S	M	T	W	T	F	S
	D/C	CC	PC	LIR	IE	
				1	2	3
4	5	6	7	8	9	10
11	12	13	14	15	16	17
18	19	20	21	22	23	24
25	26	27	28	29	30	31

JUN2025						
S	M	T	W	T	F	S
	D/C	CC	PC	LIR	IE	
1	2	3	4	5	6	7
8	9	10	11	12	13	14
15	16	17	18	19	20	21
22	23	24	25	26	27	28
29	30					

- Sprint 1 – System, Life Cycle, States, and Key Data Fields.
- Sprint 2 – Field Rules & Workflow Automation.
- Sprint 3 – Security logic, Roles, Permissions, and Formatted Outputs
- Sprint 4 – Reports & Dashboards

Legend:
- Requirement Gathering Workshops
- Configuration & Touchpoint Demonstrations
- Process Exercises Released & Feedback
- Evaluate and address feedback

Regarding the 4x4 Sprint Format, I believe most of what I've put together graphically explains this nicely and in an easy-to-understand format. If there was an outstanding question, I think it would be something to this affect: What's the difference between a dashboard, a report, and a formatted output. While implementing Veeva this is critical to understand the differences.

Dashboard

A dashboard is a mathematical algorithm that combines data into a defined manner and produces an output representative of an aggregate of like data. For example, in Veeva, one can create a dashboard that represents how many deviations were closed by their due date for a specific functional area or even the Enterprise. Generally this data would be represented by the output of a percentage. (90% of the deviations closed on time).

Report

A report is a query of a specific module with the output of generating a list of. In every inspection ever for all time, a Regulator will ask you for a list of deviations. In Veeva, that's called a report.

Formatted Output

A formatted output is a record turned into a .PDF inclusive of its attachments. From the deviation report just mentioned, a Regulator may ask to see a specific deviation record. For such a request, a Formatted Output would be provided.

Please note that validating Dashboards, Reports, and Formatted Outputs should be part of the overall user requirements at the very beginning of the project start. Project Leads, Business Leads, and GPOs should evaluate what they desire and what is required in order to be successful in all aspects of the business and compliance.

For example, regarding Dashboards...Wouldn't it be great to push a button in your eQMS to generate required metrics and data instead of the downloading of QMS data, and then manipulating that data in Excel, and then transferring that manipulation to PowerPoint for a Quality Management Review. Wouldn't that be great? Real time data discussion instead of countless hours making it ready for discussion.

To me, you'd want dashboards by department and by organization for deviations, CAPAs, Change Controls, LIRs, MRBs, PIAs, ECs. Heck, you'd want dashboards for the full of the QMS.

For example, regarding Reports. Wouldn't it be great if you validated up front all the reports you need to be inspection ready? We did this at Emergent with SAP and it saved us a lot of stress especially when the regulators were getting impatient with other requests that were not provided in a timely manner. Regarding the QMS, they were highly complementary since we had the initiative and foresight to validate the reports during the implementation of the QMS. Now don't get me wrong, if they needed something in addition, then we still needed the human resource to have the knowledge to generate it (and that was me!).

Formatted Outputs are self-explanatory and also a really amazing feature of the Veeva system. My only encouragement about the Formatted Outputs is to remember to tell Veeva you want your company logo on the output. This is critical for regulatory inspections. Another concept to keep in mind regarding the formatted outputs in Veeva is that there are two. There is the full record formatted output. This means regardless of a field or object having any data with it, it will be provided in the report. That's not something you want to provide to a Regulator because they'll ask why does this record have all of these objects associated to it without any data in them. Think about it. Then there is the Smart (this is my term for it) Formatted Output. The Smart Formatted Output only generates the .PDF of the Parent Record, the objects that have data or entries in them, and the attachments. This, and only this, is what should be provided to a Regulator upon their request.

Chapter 6
Organizational Change Management

Every successful project must have the element of Organizational Change Management. This is not to be confused with the QMS module of Change Control nor Change Management.

Organization Change Management (OCM) is a department as well as a concept. In other words, the project must have staff who are literally dedicated to OCM. And those dedicated staff must contain ideals that manage the idea of the new QMS being introduced to the masses. Always remember: Change is dynamic, abhorred by the masses, yet required by law. It's an interesting paradox that one must keep at the forefront. Also always remember, the masses have a voice and if the naysayers outnumber the non-naysayers then your project is doomed. I'm not kidding. See Chapter 9 if you don't believe me.

Organizational Change Management has the burden of coming up with methods to get the masses to adopt the new system and put the old system out of their minds. It is very difficult and, in my opinion, the most critical aspect of managing the project. From a User perspective, OCM is as simple as always keeping in mind, "what's in it for me?". If you can appeal to the User and remember to frame it in how it makes their life easier in the QMS, then you will be very successful in obtaining full adoption.

The project that inspired this volume learned that OCM was important in Phase 2. In Phase 1 I was responsible for all of the marketing strategies for change adoption and to be honest, I learned a lot which made it rewarding, but I wouldn't call my efforts successful. Mostly I was too late to that phase and the User Community were the most challenging and stubborn group I've ever dealt with. Also, I did not have relationships built with them so, I did what I could and in the end they all hated me for what was implemented. We made this an input to the Retrospective (Lessons Learned) which led to allocating additional humans specifically for OCM. I was so relieved to have additional help. Also, it's a thankless job for these wonderful humans so please remember to make an effort to thank them for their tireless efforts, wonderfully thought-out content, and strategies. I still reach out to them on occasion to catch up and also thank them for helping me be so successful for Phases 2 and 3.

Regarding strategies. Think of commercials that stand out to you and make you think about the product or service they're trying to sell you. That's OCM. Our strategies involved newsletters, email blasts, commercials, virtual and onsite awareness sessions, and my favorite, expositions. To be honest with you Dear Reader, there are plenty of OCM texts out in the market, so I'll keep this chapter short and provide the overarching strategy that served as a template for a best in class change adoption. Perhaps this will work for what you need in your project.

Organizational Change Management Adoption Strategy

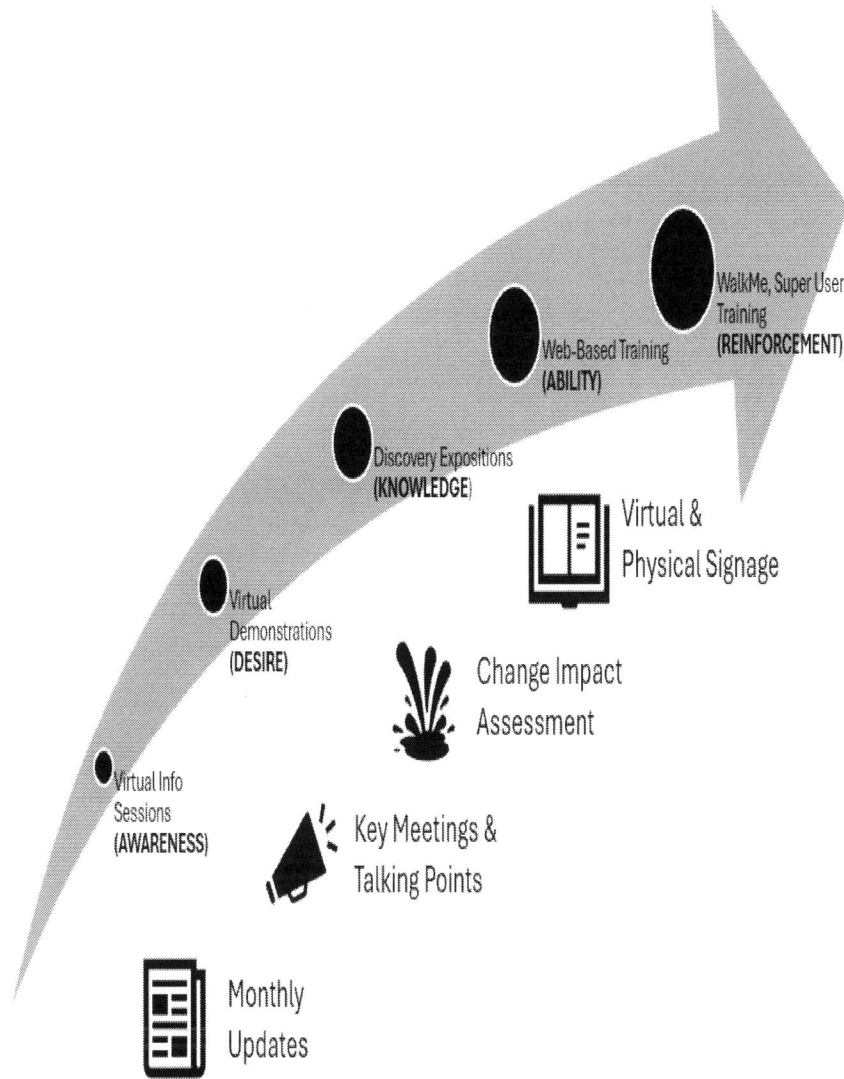

WalkMe, Super User Training
(REINFORCEMENT)

Web-Based Training
(ABILITY)

Discovery Expositions
(KNOWLEDGE)

Virtual Demonstrations
(DESIRE)

Virtual Info Sessions
(AWARENESS)

Virtual & Physical Signage

Change Impact Assessment

Key Meetings & Talking Points

Monthly Updates

Chapter 7
Hypercare

Hypercare occurs after the technical and business go live. Yes, there is a difference between a technical and business go live. The technical go-live is the date that the system is implemented, effective, and ready for the User Community to use it. That said, sometimes there are problems in the business, such as the Controlled Documents to support a module are not yet ready for release from the Document Control process. Therefore, there will be a technical go-live (system is ready to use) separate from the business go-live which is when the business is ready to use the system.

Anyway, hypercare is the next step of the project and it is defined as a period of time following the implementation of the system where an especially intensive effort is made to support the User Community through the transition. Keep in mind, in most computerized QMS implementations there is a period of time that Users must consider working in two QMSs. The one that will eventually be decommissioned and a new one. Honestly, it's quite an overwhelming experience for Users even though you may have committed extensive time and resources to the OCM strategy preparing them for this exact moment. And also remember, QMS work for most of the staff at a Pharmaceutical company is not their day-to-day job. So, even though you put in all that effort, and it seemed like they were engaged and "got it", they were probably multi-tasking and focusing their cognitive energies on what the main priority was for that given day at that given time. This is just the truth of how the business really works.

Hypercare can best be executed with multiple modalities of communication and engagement. Consider that I was the Lead for Kite, a subsidiary of Gilead. Gilead had a position that they should be active in the hypercare methodology for the entirety of the enterprise. Listen. Kite was a toxic place to work back then, and we had a lot of stubborn, immature individuals who threw temper tantrums when they didn't get their way. So, as Project Lead for Kite, my position was that we'll have Kite hypercare, and for any issues that we cannot resolve as a subsidiary organization, then we'll escalate those to Gilead hypercare. Of course, hypercare issues are tracked, trended, and evaluated for prioritization. At the end of the day, Gilead Leads were thankful for me to take on the Kite "issues" (most of which were not issues and were actually new requests – new requests do not get prioritized as hypercare topics and they do get prioritized as possible future system improvements).

For Kite hypercare we tackled it via an established email distribution list, daily office hours considering all aspects of the business and their respective timezones, an MS Teams Channel, and Frequently Asked Questions (FAQs). It was a work of art and worked beautifully. 80% of the "issues" brought to the Kite Core Team were in the lane of "how do I do XYZ?". Those are fair requests because Kite was using a system that was top to bottom for the record, and left to right for the workflow. Veeva is a multidimensional process. So, a Parent Object has to reach a specific workflow status. Then an object can be associated to the parent object. And then that associated object has to reach a certain status before the Parent can move forward. This is complicated until you do it a few times. So, many of the "issues" were "how come I can't move my parent object to the next status?".

To be honest, there were no actual "real" hypercare issues from both the Gilead side and the Kite side. We had one minor glitch with data in the change control module. Which was easily fixed with the ingestion of new data into that module. Again, it's a huge accomplishment that not many QMS implementation teams can boast about!

Well, I think that's enough for hypercare other than the marketing materials. Below is an example of how we marketed hypercare to Leaders and the User Community.

Hypercare Marketing Materials

Email Distribution List	Office Hours	MS Team's Channel	FAQs

Chapter 8
Data Migration

If you need an SOP for Data Migration head to Appendix 1. I helped establish this SOP during a recent consulting gig. Data Migration is absolutely a GMP activity so having an SOP for it makes complete logical sense. That said, I have never seen one anywhere else I've worked or audited.

I intend to keep this chapter short.

Stated simply, data migration is migrating the totality of the data from one eQMS to the newly implemented eQMS.

Data in this context represents all characters within all fields of the record, list of value selections, 100% of the audit trail, comments to the audit trail, and attachments and course from all versions of each QMS module. Also, you will want to entertain the idea of a short and long term strategies for the data migration effort. For example, deviation records will have a short term strategy. The best strategy is to close all of the still open records because it's easier and costs less to migrate closed records. Develop a strategy for each QMS module. I have strategies for each module but it costs more than this text book!

In order to successfully migrate the data, one must map all of the data from the old system field by field, value by value, workflow by workflow, and all attachments to the new and potentially like for like data in the new system. This effort is tracked via very complex Excel spreadsheets and tested in triplicate to ensure no hiccups or data errors when the actual migration takes place.

What happens if in the new system, the data does not line up from the old system? In the Veeva process this would be considered "legacy" data. There is something that all pharmaceutical companies need to know about Veeva legacy data. Veeva legacy data is populated in the Veeva Legacy object. That's cool, except if you were expecting that you would be able to google-like search on legacy data – at the time of this writing you can't. What you can do is run a report on the legacy object. Anyway, it's very critical to understand this before you migrate the data. Because if you lose your reportability and query-ability on something that you needed it for, for inspection readiness, for quality management review, for deviation trending, or for just for Work Center Team (WCT) management, then you lose it. And then you're stuck trying to figure out work arounds. We were very fortunate that we had someone like me ask the right questions to ensure that there were no glitches in the matrix this way.

Also, for some reason, probably due to conserved heads of quality who are averse to risk, companies make the mistake of hinging go-live on data being successfully at the same time as the technical go-live. Here's a new way to think about this. Execute the data migration after the technical go-live. It makes so much more sense to do it like this. It's more cost effective because you're working with the real system and not the simulated environment (so it cuts way down on the steps and the number of resources completing the work). And from a systems position, it's much easier to place data into the live system than in the less controlled environment. Also, because it's more controlled it's actually safer to do it this way. What does "safer" mean – It means it ensures 100% integrity of the data. It's also simpler (and simplicity keeps ensures integrity of the data and breeds compliance to data integrity!).

And of course, Data Migration requires a change control. Please continue to the next chapter.

Chapter 9
Project Related Change Controls

To start us off I'll casually remind you, Dear Reader, that this volume was inspired by a four-year project owned by Gilead but managed both by Gilead and Kite. As I've mentioned, in this scenario, I'm the Global Program Owner of Deviation, CAPA, Effectiveness Verification, and Change Control. I'm also the Interim Head of the QMS. And from a quality perspective, I own the Kite Agile-QMS system. Gilead, as the Parent company owns the Veeva system, the one to be implemented. Therefore, they own all of the primary Change Controls to implement the project and they include staff such as myself from the Kite side to review and approve the Gilead change controls. On the Kite side, we also were required to own change controls to ensure we controlled any changes made to Agile or anything else that required a change control such as the migration of data from Agile-QMS to Veeva-QMS. I want to take a moment to highlight some project issues we ran into from the data migration perspective, how we controlled it, and a few other nuggets we ran into that were fun surprises.

Please recall that Phase 1 of the project implemented the Quality Risk Management (QRM) module. You might be shocked to learn that there were no Kite Change Controls for Phase 1. There was one Gilead Change Control. Prior to go-live with QRM in Veeva, QRM was managed via SmartSheet and Veeva-Document Control. What this means is that there was no validated quality management system for QRM. It was managed by one individual, in a SmartSheet, and actual risk assessments were managed in Veeva-Document Control. The thought and the decision (not made by me) was that all risk assessments in Veeva-Document Control could remain there and did not have to migrate to the new system. They were "living documents" as I was told and that was the sole reason for that decision. (Even though it was the wrong decision). So, because there was no former QMS for QRM and because there was no data to migrate, there were no Kite Change Controls. What about the documents and the curricula Mike? Smart question! Those require document change controls and not QMS change controls.

Phase 2 of the project implemented the "heavy hitters": Deviation, CAPA, Effectiveness Check, Change Control, Product Complaints, Laboratory Investigation Reports, Issue Escalations, and the Regulatory Notification Assessment (RNA). The RNA Quality Action replaced what was known in Agile-QMS as the Biological Product Deviation Report (BPDR) and Additional Information (AI) record. Also, Issue Escalations was a paper-based QMS. Other context is that Deviation, Change Control, and LIR had versioned in Agile. I hope that you can already see some of the complexities that I and my IT partner were facing when it came to decommissioning the Agile-QMS.

In Phase 2, my IT partner and I managed four change controls in addition to reviewing and approving the Gilead change controls. In the Issue Escalation space, we decided to migrate the paper-based Issue Escalations as an archive to forever be referenced in the meta-data in Veeva-Document Control of the Issue Escalation SOP. We made this decision because the paper-based format in no way whatsoever could be field mapped to the new record that was to go-live. Therefore, any paper-based open or in-process Issue Escalations would be force fit into the new record upon go live. To be precise, closed Issue Escalations were migrated as an archive to Veeva-Document Control, and any open or in-process Issue Escalations would be opened as a record in Veeva-QMS. Of course anything that was on paper, was attached to the record for posterity. We managed this in one Change Control that the Global Program Owner of Issue Escalation managed with myself as the Quality Approver. In this manner, we ensured data integrity and also complete traceability for any future requests from Regulators. It was a simple, yet comprehensive solution.

In the Laboratory Investigation Record (LIR) space, we learned that there were two versions of LIR. And in the first version, there were only 30 or so records. And in version 1, it was nothing like the to-be record therefore field mapping to the new record was not viable. Like Issue Escalation, we decided that data migration for version 1 of LIR was also going to be an archive. We managed that with a separate change control owned by the GPO of LIR and me as the Quality Approver. The rest of the nearly 10,000 LIRv2 records were field mapped and migrated under our Kite "heavy hitter" data migration change control.

Obviously, we had a change control to manage decommissioning the Kite QMS modules in scope of Phase 2. And our last change control was to manage the data migration of the QMS modules in the scope of Phase 2.

We applied the same strategies to the Phase 3 modules in scope.

Why am I telling you this? I'm telling you this because most firms decide to place all of these activities into one change control. My goodness, what a nightmare that is. First, that means the change control will be open for a very long time. And it's ok to segment the changes into phases and then tie each of the records together. You might find this note to be funny too. Three of these changes were in the Agile-QMS, which then migrated to the Veeva-QMS. And then one of the changes was solely in Veeva-QMS. That's fun to think about (actually take a moment to think about that!). Anyway, don't make the mistake of trying to control these changes as one change. Think about what makes the most logical sense and always think about change control with the end in mind. What does success of this change actually look like? (And keep it simple!)

Chapter 10
Critical Lessons Learned

Critical Lesson 1: Determine Your Training Strategy in the Project's Infancy

In a Quality by Delitala book, titled, "Solve Problems Like a Pro", I write about my time as the Head of Training and a problem I solved in this space.

Here's the problem:

> *All projects and staff trying to accomplish anything in the QMS space always forget to plan for Training. Training is the last stop and is the most downstream of all the quality management systems. It's often forgotten about in any of the planning phases for all things ranging from simple SOP revisions to large projects that want to revise the full of the QMS when they're implementing new computerized systems for example.*

For context, in Phase 1 which implemented just the QRM module, we nearly missed the deadline to have the User Community trained at go-live. If the staff were not fully trained at go-live it meant that some sites would not have any trained users to manage risk at their site. This is a big problem, and it was strange for us because we had planned for this and even included contingency plans. I think the biggest thing to know in this space is that we had a very small community to train: 36 individuals. The overarching problem what that our training strategy had a gargantuan amount of instructor led training (ILT), five of them per role, and those 36 staff each had 12 ILTs to attend (plus, you know, their day job), and there was only one instructor. Because we missed the mark and could not get all staff trained in time it of course made headlines (it was escalated) with the highest level of leadership.

Next, we're implementing this massive new QMS at a time at Kite where the company was about to ramp up production and resources by over 50% of the current reality. The Leadership made it very clear to me as the Project Lead by calling me out in a Quality Management Review. The highest leader in Manufacturing, paused during the meeting, pointed at me and said, "Mike Delitala, you will not impact my department with the implementation of Next Gen QMS". Of course, what she meant was that they were ramping up production, and also she meant, can you please tell me what the training strategy was going to be so that we all can be sure we're not going to be negatively impacted by this event. It was fair feedback even if it was the wrong forum to provide it, and even if it was provided emotionally and with the use of incorrect words. All feedback is a gift and we all have to do our best to interpret the real message.

In the next leadership meeting where I was to provide an update on Next Gen QMS, that same leader asked me if I knew what the training strategy was going to be. Because obviously it could be the same as the training strategy for QRM deployment. I honestly did not know the answer. And from that point forward, I made it my mission to understand the answer. The problem was that this was March and go-live for Phase 2 was set for December. The real problem was that it was not my decision and it was absolutely Gilead's decision. In any regard, I started to follow up with the Gilead leads to see if we could at least start the conversation. No luck. In June, this topic was escalated to the CEO of Kite and I was pulled into a very uncomfortable meeting where I received a lot of adverse feedback and also, "why don't you know the answer to this question?". In my mind, "how come you don't understand that I'm the Kite lead and have no decisions related to the Gilead business". Anyway…

I set up a meeting with the Gilead Head of the QMS who ultimately was the responsible person for the implementation of the system. I voiced my Leader's concerns and concluded with, "If we can't start discussing this at the Project Core Team and attempt to land somewhere, then I believe I will have to use the decision-making model and escalate it to the Steering Committee". His eyes were wide for a moment, and then he agreed – "You're absolutely right Mike. Let's get this conversation started". I said, "Thank you, and I'll be vying for a more modern approach to training. As in, how about mini web-based trainings (WBT). If we go the route of ILTs, then we're never going to make it on time.". And then I told him about the QRM debacle and from that moment forward, he became my biggest advocate to influence WBT, which of course is self-paced and can be monitored for progress towards completion.

A week later, he and I were able to convince the Heads of Training that this was the best, most modern, solution to ensure all users receive the correct training to get access while having the least impact on resources. Win-Win! I then went on a mission to put together marketing materials for this glorious decision which included, for the one Leader asking for it, how much time will it take a person to train to get their access.

The next week a specific meeting was called with my supervisor, and my supervisor's supervisor, as well as the top Manufacturing Leadership. They put together a PowerPoint presentation that was at least 50 slides long, and in this meeting used my full name 10 times. "Mike Delitala is an inadequate Project Lead". "Mike Delitala is unable to answer simple questions such as how long will it take a user to train". "Mike Delitala is ignoring the User Community and has not considered any one of our requests to make a record the way we want it". And so on and so forth. None of it was true of course and in my own mind I wondered why these individuals didn't come to me first. Yes, that's the definition of Toxic. Anyway, after about 15 minutes of this ridicule, which was horrific, the Leader looked at me dead in the face, and said, "So, Mike Delitala, what do you have to say about all of this". "Yes, thank you for bringing me into the meeting. If you'll allow me to share my screen, I have the answer to your question. By the way, to get to the answer to your question, as the Project Lead, I had to nearly escalate this to the Project Steering Committee. Please keep in mind that this is actually Gilead's decision and not mine. But after several months and several attempts to get you this decision, I think you'll be very happy. For the average user it will take as little as two hours. For the user who has multiple accesses, it could take them up to 5 hours of self-paced, easy, web-based trainings plus read and understand of the new controlled documents such as SOPs and Work Instructions".

As one might imagine, jaws dropped to the floor. The VP of Compliance finally spoke up and said in his very stoic way, "Excellent news! Is there anything else we can do for you today?". And just like that, I was a hero and the meeting came to its natural conclusion. I'm laughing because I can't even make this stuff up even if I tried and I also have works of Fiction so that's why it's funny!

The lesson learned here: Determine what your training strategy is in the infancy of the project. It's okay if it changes later and expect and predict that it will. Do this because every project's natural tendency is to determine it too late in the implementation. I'd say do it first. You can do it in the middle too. Just don't do it last!

By the way, this escalation made it to the VP of Quality. And what happened next has become legendary. The first thing that happened after this meeting (where I won) was that the quality department for a reason I still do not understand mutinied. They refused all participation in the project. I thought I was screwed. The funny thing is, that after this horrendous escalation meeting, I finally broke under the pressure. I had been working with my Kite coach, who is an amazing individual and our session was right after this meeting. I almost did not go to the coaching session because my body was twitching and convulsing and I was soaked in sweat. This is not normal for me and I thought I would have to go to the hospital.

So, I arrive to the coaching session and she can see that I'm out of sorts. With sobbing tears, I mutter something to the affect, "I'm sorry I'm late. I have to go. Something horrible just happened". And in all of her wisdom, she told me to stay, and I've got you. Let's talk it out. She helped me with my inner dialogue on all of this by helping me realize that no matter what happens, I have a great team, I myself am committed to this, and there is no way in hell that we don't go live when we say we're going to go live. So, "what's the problem Mike?". Great question. The problem seems to be that now matter how hard I work for this company, they just don't value my contributions and how I actually have given them everything they've asked in this project. The next thing that happened was that my coach gave me an invaluable tool that literally changed my life and how I would manage the project moving forward. The tool or method is called Evoking a Quality of Presence. I mastered it overnight and then I became a superhero in the next escalation meeting where I course corrected the whole project towards a seamless implementation. Refer to Appendix 3 for the method. You're welcome.

I mastered the method over night. With the Quality functions no longer on my side, I did not panic and instead reached out to the Manufacturing Project Management department. They too realized my dilemma and much to my surprise invited me to their monthly Project Update department. Here's the kicker: All Quality functions are also represented at this monthly update meeting. To be honest, I did not have a plan. I did not know what was going to happen but I had my new super power of "calm" and I'm the only one on Planet Kite who had answer for the Next Gen QMS project so what was there to be nervous about at this point.

The meeting starts and the meeting chair hands the mic over to me to provide an update. I have all of my marketing materials, I give them the latest update, the new training strategy, how much time it will take, and what's still left to complete in the project. Then the best thing happened. One of the Manufacturing site Project Managers comes in to the meeting with a question. "So, Mike, thanks for the amazing update. I'm over wondering what do you need from us. And, is there anything we can help you with?". I get goose bumps all over because what that Project Manager just did was give me the option. Having the option I do a *Mike thing* and I wax poetic for about 30 seconds. I say something to the affect of: "Thank you for the question. I'm new to this forum so please forgive me if I stumble and bumble a bit. You know, I'm just looking around the room and I see that all of the Sites are represented here by Project Managers. Is that correct?". They all nod their head yes. "Excellent. Well, I don't know about you, but if I'm a Project Manager at a site, then it feels like to me that the Project Managers at the site level would want to manage the tasks that are site-specific.". I see them all nodding their heads yes so I go for the kill shot. "So, if that's part of the remit of this forum, then I'd like to hear from each of the Project Managers on what they think". They all came in unanimously and agreed with me 100%. (this is legendary!)

The Quality departments were immediately upset and also 100% against. Why? What does it mean? It means two things. One, Quality will now be told what to do by Manufacturing (and that's never supposed to happen). Two, it meant that little, junior, Associate Director Mike, in one 30 minute meeting was able to get the full manufacturing department to align with him. It's a genius move. And the Head of Quality told me it was a genius move. He also dropped some eff bombs on me, like how in the heck did it get to this point? I agreed with him. And then he did me a solid. He formed a Quality Champion's forum. Where a Quality Leader from each site was required to join my team and "actually participate and you will help this guy get this done"! Bam. Just like that, I now had all of manufacturing and all of quality aligned. No one gives me credit for this, by the way. This story is true and remarkable, and it paved the way for the successful implementation of the system. As in there were no more naysayers nor doomsdayers and everyone played nice and were actually good teammates for a change!

The critical lesson of that story is that **In the throes of a mutiny by Quality, make Manufacturing your best friend!**

Critical Lesson 2: Know the generational status of your core team

Seems like an obvious lesson. For me, I had not realized that the world had changed. Gen Z. Millennials. I have never really paid much attention to it. Well, I had a team of millennials. They were super smart and extremely talented, but I did not know that I needed to hold their hands across all of the finish lines. Back then, I was managing projects to due dates and milestones with periodic check ins to see if they needed help. After about the third check-in to see if they needed help I realized, to my detriment, that the they did not have the same experiences as I've had and also that there was no level of onboarding that would help them complete the work. One bold Program Owner even came into the meeting and said, "What is it specifically you want us to do?".

I was in shock, tried not to show it, and said, "great question. I have an idea. Let's all meet in a conference room where we can brainstorm and whiteboard together". Apparently that response was not the right response because I didn't acknowledge their feelings.

So, anyway, get to know the generational status of your team because it helps you cater your message in the right way for them, and also it will help with your own expectations about how you need to manage the priorities and the tasks.

That individual ended up complaining that I hurt their feelings because I was holding them accountable to a due date, really a significant project milestone. So, for the best year of my career, I received a does-not-meet-expectations and also was put on a PIP. Since I try to find the positive in all things, it was actually a good thing because then I became a subject matter expert on Emotional Intelligence and Tact. Also, it serves as one of the variables that has led to the Quality by Delitala books and my own company.

Critical Lesson 3: Become friends with the Public Affairs department

Since this is a book on Quality in the Pharmaceutical Industry, I think this metaphor will land for you. Remember that first time you wrote a deviation and handed it to your quality approver thinking you did a really good job? Remember that feeling? Yeah, that's what it's like to work with Public Affairs. They speak their own language, they know what they want, they know what good looks like, but they don't know how to articulate it back to you. I hope you're laughing. One of my charges in this project was the Head of Quality mandated that I have virtual signage on the public monitors which hit all of the manufacturing sites. To be clear, he wanted to advertise the project in a medium that all sites would be able to see. It made sense. Except, I had to work with Public Affairs. It's funny because I didn't think we were advanced enough as a company to even have that department. I had the OCM team craft me up some nice advertisements and then provided them to Public Affairs in a meeting I set up with them. Well, three months go by and I still do not have virtual signs. I'm now receiving all kinds of adverse feedback from Public Affairs because afterall they should have been involved in the project from the start. Just in case it's not clear, this is 100% a Quality project and 0% to do with Public Affairs. It was escalated to the Head of Quality, which was a good thing because he was about to fire me because I had no signs up anywhere and he had made the request after all!

The lesson here is to make friends with your Public Affairs department early in the project in the event you are asked to advertise globally. They're actually really nice people and it will be fun for your to learn the language of that group. They have all kinds of interesting unwritten rules!

Critical Lesson 4: You can never have enough communication or updates about the status of the project.

I'll just say this. At the end of the project, even though I landed it right first time, under budget, and on time, that I was actually eliminated from the company on the day it technically went live. I over communicated. I under communicated. I didn't communicate the right things. All of which was not true but that was the perception and other people's perceptions are your reality. Don't forget it.

I'm super proud of it no matter what and this volume demonstrates my expertise in this area and no one can ever take that way.

The real lesson to learn here is rely heavily on your OCM team for the right communication and ensure your leadership is well informed of the communication plan and strategy. Accept their feedback no matter what!

Chapter 12
Retrospective

The shortest chapter of the book.

A Retrospective is a Lessons Learned activity.

We do this so that we implement solutions to problems encountered in the previous phase so that we do not have the same problem in the next phase.

A best-in-class project will always require a Retrospective before starting the next phase of the project. (but no one thinks like this!) I mandate this for all projects I lead.

Chapter 13
Miscellaneous yet Equally Important Nuggets That did not Make it in Other Chapters

Important Nugget 1: When there is a Parent company, the Document Revision strategy must take into account the Parent documents and the subsidiary documents.

In this case, Gilead owned all of the Global System Agnostic documents. Kite still had to maintain their own controlled documents to account for Kite specific requirements related to immunotherapy and associated training. In any regard, below is an example of how we messaged leaders on this subject.

Document Timeline and Key Milestones

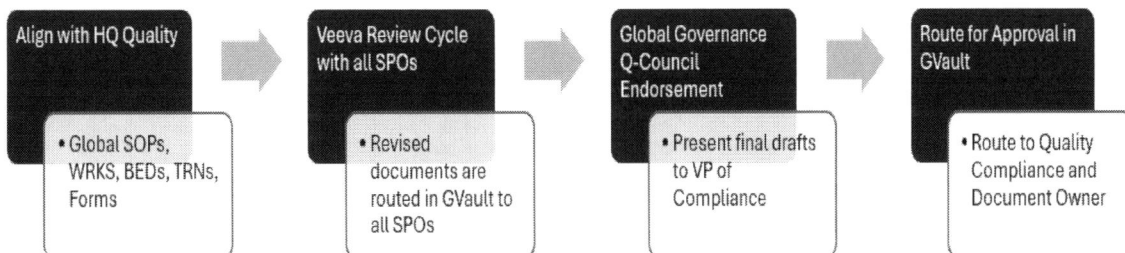

Align with HQ Quality
- Global SOPs, WRKS, BEDs, TRNs, Forms

Veeva Review Cycle with all SPOs
- Revised documents are routed in GVault to all SPOs

Global Governance Q-Council Endorsement
- Present final drafts to VP of Compliance

Route for Approval in GVault
- Route to Quality Compliance and Document Owner

Timeline for each step is input on the line

Important Nugget 2: The Document Revision strategy must be representative of the Parent and subsidiary hierarchy. This applies to the training curricula as well. It's best to represent this graphically. (like the below).

Document Infrastructure Involves Global SOPs and WRKs by Company and Module

Veeva QMS General Use SOP	Module Specific Use SOPs	Entity Specific Use SPOs
• Gilead Owned • Application Level • System Specific • Global	• Gilead Owned • Global, per module	• Parent entities • Subsidiary entities (owned by subsidiary)

Important Nugget 3: When you have to deploy a strategy where Non-Quality departments are more your friends than the quality department, then be prepared to provided a detailed analysis of what you specifically need from them...

Because remember...these are hard working folks who have a really difficult day job to do and they are hardly thanked for it. Yet, they are always ready and willing to put in the extra effort. These are truly extraordinary people. Below is a template that I used quite successfully to have them help me drive the project to completion from an execution perspective. Maybe it will help you in your future implementation endeavors.

Site-Specific Activities to Complete the Implementation

SITE-SPECIFIC TASKS							
Role Mapping by Module	Super User Training	Curriculum Management	Local Document Revisions	Create Reports & Views	Site Hypercare Support	Open Record Migration	Exposition Support

A few assumptions to consider with the tasks:
1. It is assumed that we will likely have the same training strategy as last year (mostly ILT and R/U).
2. There is a limited budget for travel.
3. All Leads from all Entities will be working together this year towards the alignment with the Parent company.
4. Many of the staff who need access to the Phase 3 modules most likely have some kind of access to Gvault QMS (so, it's not as big of a lift in Phase 3 as it was in Phase 2).

Note to the Reader: In my actual marketing materials I used the bubbles icon that you see next to the assumptions above. This is because our bubbles were popped in each of these categories. For example, we basically had an unlimited budget for Phase 2. And because we spent so much money on travel and expositions (I spent $24000 in Amsterdam alone!) we were told to come up with solutions where we spent no money!

Epilogue

Some of you who are reading this volume will be quick to point out that there are some things I have left out of this volume. And for those who think that you're super smart and you're correct. I intentionally left out Validation. Validation is a volume unto itself. Also, each company has their own way of being compliant to the laws that govern validation. If I were to have placed my tenets of computerized validation in this volume, I believe it would be scrutinized to the nth degree and there really is no reason for that.

I also left out tenets of Project Management. As a PMP, I subscribe to a very specific way of managing a project. Again, there are so many resources in that space why would I? The point of this volume is to give you a best-in-class recipe to implement a computerized QMS. I think I'm a pretty good quality lead, business lead, and project manager. That said, you can just hire Ben Riblett because he's the best ever and will remain that way to infinity.

I also left out specific dashboards, reports, and formatted outputs. I'm well aware of what a computerized QMS can do. In fact, the vision should be that you no longer have to download data for quality management review and instead just open your QMS, demonstrate what the data shows, and have a real continuous improvement conversation in real-time. (No one thinks like this!).

I also left out our exposition strategy and the glorious details that make up a show for production purposes. That, my friends, is another *Mike thing* and well, you just have to experience it. I could write about it. There are videos of it that I no longer possess. And, on that note I'll be humble but be proud of the fact that I received 1000 five-star ratings for my performance. Not too shabby!

I also left out a major aspect of today's modern QMS. That's Data Sciences, Data Analytics, and Artificial Intelligence. I left this out intentionally. It's an entire volume to itself but the reality is that each pharmaceutical company must go through the pain of figuring out what they actually want or need in these spaces. When I first arrived to Kite, I had no way of understanding with data what the health or pulse of my QMS was. I immediately tracked down Data Sciences and we ideated 40 Tableau reports together. I estimated that by creating these 40 reports, we saved the company over $100,000 a month because before those reports, staff were downloading data to Excel, cleansing it, manipulating it, and then transferring it to .PPT presentations. Good grief! It's so much easier now to do this with Spotfire or Tableau.

In any regard, I left other key concepts out too. If you're in need of them, please contact me through LinkedIn and I will be happy to help solve your computerized quality management system problems.

Remember, keep it simple. Simplicity breeds compliance.

Appendix 1
Data Migration Concept & Application

Note to the Reader:

Data Migration from one or from several computerized systems into the intended computerized system is usually a process governed by IT with quality oversight. It is always controlled via the change control process and in all places, and in all events except once, I have never observed the process to be controlled through a standard operating procedure.

That said, I consulted at one sophisticated place where the most amazing IT Leader I have ever met, demanded excellence always, and as such required that I write him a Data Migration SOP prior to us even considering initiating the implementation of Veeva.

What follows is that SOP as bonus material. This is not normal so it will be your choice to either manage data migration as a business task with quality oversight in a change control and a validation package, or to follow a standard operating procedure.

It is a GMP activity, so trust me, it makes perfect sense to have a procedure in place.

Chapter 9: Bonus Material: Quality by Delitala Procedure for Data Migration

1. **Purpose**
    1.1. This procedure defines the steps and the processes for the migration of electronic records, data, and metadata from one computerized system to another computerized system. (Or for multiple computerized systems into the intended computerized system).
2. **Scope**
    2.1. This procedure applies to all electronic records, data, and metadata from computerized systems used within GxP processes.
3. **References – N/A**
4. **Definitions**

Term	Definition
Computerized System	A set of software and hardware components which together provide functionalities to create, modify, maintain, archive, retrieve, or transmit in digital form.
Electronic Record	Any combination of text, graphics, data, audio, visual, or other information representing digital forms that are created, modified, maintained, archived, retrieved or distributed by a computer system.
Metadata	Data that describe the attributes of other data and provide context and meaning to some aspect of the electronic record.

5. Roles & Responsibilities

Role	Responsibility
Business Process Owner (BPO)	• An identified individual or function who owns the business aspect of the computerized system. • Contributes to the Data Migration Plan ensuring that electronic data, records, and metadata are transferred accurately and completely. • Execute data migration and data migration verification tasks as defined in the Data Migration Plan.
System Technology Owner (STO)	• Authors the Data Migration Plan and Data Migration Summary Report. • Manages the Data Migration process. • Executes data migration tasks as defined in the Data Migration Plan.
System Technology Representative (STR)	• Authors the Data Migration Plan and Data Migration Summary Report. • Executes data migration tasks as defined in the Data Migration Plan.
Quality	• Contributes to the Data Migration Plan ensuring that electronic data, records, and metadata are transferred accurately, completely, and compliantly. • Executes data migration verification tasks as defined in the Data Migration Plan. • Retains and archives records.

6. Equipment / Materials – N/A

7. Safety – N/A

8. Procedure

8.1. Data Migration Planning

8.1.1. The STO assigns a STR to author the Data Migration Plan (DMP)

8.1.2. The STR partners with the BPO and Quality to obtain User Requirements.

8.1.3. The Data Migration Plan must contain the following:

DMP Component	Description & Instructions
Source System Description	• A brief description of the source system which includes the system name, application version number, and a high-level overview of the purpose of the system.
Target System Description	• A brief description of the target system, including system name, application version number, and a high-level overview of the purpose of the system.

DMP Component	Description & Instructions
Business Process and User Scope	<ul><li>Describe the scope of the business processes including the data or records, or product lines, or client base.</li><li>Describe the user population impacted or connected to the data migration event including geographical locations, sites, and departments.</li></ul>
Scope of Records	<ul><li>Describe the scope of electronic records, data, and metadata to be migrated including:<ul><li>Record types</li><li>Record scope such as for a specific site or department</li><li>Record ranges (such as magnitude and date range)</li></ul></li></ul>
Record Retention Policy	<ul><li>Identify the retention period for the records in scope</li><li>Calculate the date by which the records must be retained.</li></ul>
Migration Method	<ul><li>Describe in explicit detail the steps and tasks required for migrating records, data, and metadata manually or with an automated tool, or a combination of both.</li><li>Identify any vendor-supplied tools that will be used for the event.</li><li>Automated tools must be validated and controlled via the Change Control process.</li></ul>
Migration Verification Method	<ul><li>Describe in explicit detail the steps and tasks required for verification of the accuracy and completeness of the migrated records, data, and metadata either manually or via an automated tool.</li><li>Identify any vendor-suppled tools that will be used for the migration event.</li><li>Automated tools must be validated and controlled via the Change Control process.</li><li>If the migration verification team will be verifying less than 100% of the migrated records, then the sample size will be documented, explained, and justification will be provided.</li><li>Define in explicit detail the approach for documenting verification results as well as how exceptional conditions will be handled and documented.</li></ul>
Migration Schedule	<ul><li>A detailed and reasonable schedule will be documented.</li><li>Ensure all planned down times for all computerized systems are noted in the schedule.</li><li>Communicate all down times well in advance to the user population and department heads so that department heads enforce business contingency plans. **(NOTE: This is particularly critical for all processes with an input into Disposition of final product).**</li></ul>
Communication Plan	<ul><li>Define the plan for communication before, during, and after migration.</li><li>Ensure the plan includes details such as the timing, audience, method, author, and the method of each communication.</li></ul>

DMP Component	Description & Instructions
Migration Records	• Define the migration records that will be retained. • Define the location where each record will be retained.

8.2. DMP Approval

8.2.1. DMPs must be approved by Quality, the BPO, and the STO.

8.3. DMP Execution

8.3.1. STO or STR will manage the execution of the activities defined in the DMP.

8.4. Data Migration Summary Report (DMSR)

8.4.1. The STR authors a DMSR documenting the results of the execution of the DMP. The report will contain the following elements:

8.4.1.1. Summary of records migrated.

8.4.1.2. Summary of verification activities.

8.4.1.3. Summary and status of migration issues and their resolution.

8.4.1.4. Explanation of all exceptional conditions and their impact to the migration event.

8.5. DMSR Approval

8.5.1. DMSR reports must be approved by Quality, BPO, and STO.

8.6. Data Migration Records

8.6.1. Data Migration records are governed by Change Control.

8.6.2. Documentation of Data Migration will be contained in the following:

8.6.2.1. Change Control

8.6.2.2. Data Migration Plan

8.6.2.3. Records as extracted from source systems

8.6.2.4. Print outs of records extracted from the target system

8.6.2.5. Verification reports or logs

8.6.2.6. Exceptional conditions and their resolution

8.6.2.7. DMSR

Appendix 2
Bonus Material – What is Quality and How do you Instill it?

In 2025 I was given the privilege to present to the American Strategic Portfolio Management in Life Sciences – West Coast. Technically speaking, it was my first speaking gig following a 30-year career in the Pharmaceutical Industry. The conference manager and producer said "yes" to me in large part because of my Quality by Delitala books. Initially, they asked me to speak on Total Quality Management (TQM) as it relates to Quality Assurance and Compliance. I told them that's definitely something I could speak on. I queried though: "Why TQM? TQM is great theoretically and conceptually but it's hardly effective in application". They responded with, "We have a great many Project Managers in attendance at this event and many of them have voiced they could use a run down on 'what quality is particularly in the areas of QA and Compliance". "I see", I said. "Having been a project manager for many projects myself, I believe the feedback being provided by other PMs is, 'what is quality, and how do we build it into project management". "If you're interested in that being the primary subject, then I can present Quality by Design and how it instills quality". They really liked the idea and I thought the materials presented at the conference would make for a great ending to this four part series in which I've highlighted the Health, Control, Lifecycle, and the how-to implement the full of the QMS. With that, here are my speaking notes and slides for:

(Note: It's also on YouTube here: https://youtu.be/RRZAodJZODk)

What is Quality and how do you Instill it?

(1) What to Say...	(1) Content
Today's presentation will provide the framework to implement quality in all pharma companies. • Simplicity breeds compliance. • And today's presentation will provide in a very easy to understand format, how quality is implemented in pharma companies. • By the end of the presentation I'll actually have it all in process flow diagram format. • Now, I say pharma companies with an exception: Medical Device Companies. • I'm not a big fan of CFR820 simply because it's not for me. So, if you're a part of a Medical Device Company, I mean you no offense. • That said, this presentation, in some part, may not be for you. • If you're a drug substance, drug product, small molecule, biologics, or small molecule company, then this presentation is for you.	What is *Quality* and how do you instill it? Today's presentation will provide the framework to implem quality in all pharma companies. Simplicity breeds compliance.

(2) What to Say...

Instilling quality starts with ICHQ10 & The Quality Manual.

A short note regarding *compliance*.

Anyone want to take a stab what it means to be compliant?

- Often times, there is a problem. And less experienced staff run to their quality partner screaming, "we're out of compliance" "oh gosh, we're out of compliance". Anyone ever have this happen to them?

Here's what compliance means:

1. Compliance means following the regulations (the law).
2. Compliance also means meeting your own internal standards which are the company's policies and standard operating procedures.

Now, why does quality start with ICH Q10?

- Because the Regulators say so.
- Basically, the introduction of ICHQ10 says, based on the phase of your product, if you meet the requirements (which they disguise as "guidance") herein, then you'll be compliant and more importantly you'll have a product that is safe for patients and of high quality.
- I would argue that ICH Q10 is Quality by Design (QbD) in detail.
- In fact, I do make this argument in Quality by Delitala Volume 1 – The Quality Manual (and in that volume, I give you The Quality Manual).

(2) Content

(3) What to Say Part 1...
ICHQ10 Requires the Following…   • Present aspects of the Table that are of interest   • After presenting the table, then say: • This is just the start of how you implement quality at a pharma company.   • The next sections of this presentation detail how to instill it.   • I just want this to be clear…Implementing a Quality Manual does not mean you have implemented quality.

(3) Content Part 1

ICH Q10 Requires the Following...

What is needed...	Why...
Introduction	Defines who the company is and what they manufacture.
Purpose	Describes that it is the governing document and describes the state of control.
Scope	Informs of how in-sources vs out-sourced activities are managed.
Company Mission	Defines what the company is committed to.
Quality Policy	Details the quality responsibilities and culture of quality.
Management Responsibility	Accountability (because the law says so).
Quality Unit Responsibility	Details the quality responsibilities and culture of quality.
Document Hierarchy	Defines the levels and categories of documents and records to support the QMS.
Continuous Improvement	Defines the methodology by which the company will continually improve.
Outsourced Activities	Self-explanatory
QMS & Quality Processes	Defines the extent of the QMS and all quality processes (Dev, CAPA, etc...)
Knowledge Management	Next
Quality Plan	A detailed list of tasks with due dates and milestones on how to check on quality.

(3) What to Say Part 2...
Regarding Knowledge Management – Anyone have Knowledge Management as a Quality System at their firm? I've only seen it once.   PREDICTION: Hurry up. Make the case. You need a knowledge management quality system.   • Why: Because it's the law per ICHQ10.   • Here's an example from by Quality by Delitala Volume 1

(3) Content Part 2
Callirrhoe has a Knowledge Management program, policy, and system that ensures there is a systematic approach to acquire, analyze, store, and disseminate information related to products, manufacturing, processes, and components. This is achieved in great part via Callirrhoe's Quality Management Review and Callirrhoe's Executive Management Quality Review. Additionally, Callirrhoe publishes a monthly quality newsletter that reaches the full organization. Sources of knowledge management are Callirrhoe's personnel, designs of experiments, technology transfers, process validation, experience, innovation, continuous improvement activities, change management, industry journals, industry forums, and scientific publications.

(4) What to say...

Next: Define the Firms Product & Phase of Product
This is critical.
Whenever I land a consulting gig, or start at a new firm, one of the first things I attempt to understand is
    1. What kind of product (s) do we have?
    2. What phase of the lifecycle are we in for each?
 	
   • If you don't know this, then you can't be compliant.
   • The reason for understanding this is so that you can be sure you're following the right regulations.
   • Whether it's CBER, CDER, both, or gene therapy regulations, you have to know what the product is in order to be able to comply to the right rules.
   • I know that's basic, but companies get this grossly incorrect.
   • At the last place I worked, I was sorry to inform them that they were a gene therapy company and that they were grossly out of compliance to gene therapy laws. I informed them to my detriment. And that's all I have to say about that.

(4) Content

Next: Define the Firm's Product & Phase of Product

(5) What to say...

Next: Define all regulations applicable to product & facility
   • Often times, companies use all of the regulations for all regulatory bodies and build them into the tome of their policies and procedures.
   • That's overly rigorous, extremely short sighted, and not simple at all. Therefore, there is too large of a burden to bear within quality and it's like everything is a mistake.
   • So, only comply to the laws that you need to comply to.
   • And keep it simple.

(5) Content

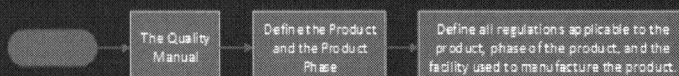

Next: Define all regulations applicable to product & facility

(6) What to say…

Next: Complete a Gap Assessment

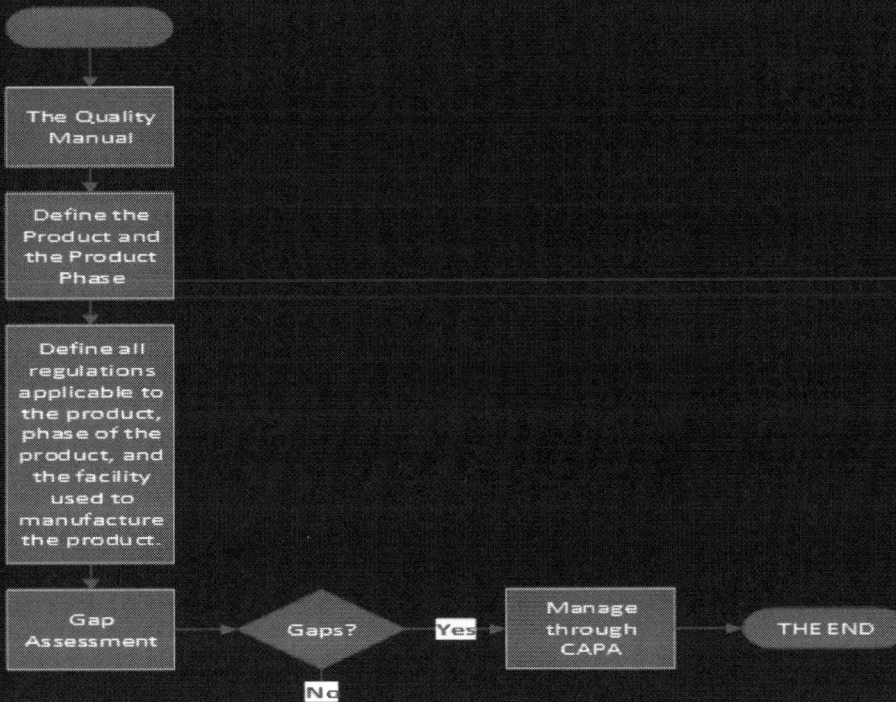

- Now, it's likely you're at stage where you have all the Policies and Procedures in place.   That's great.
- Because the next step is to complete a gap assessment comparing the existing body of documents to the defined laws based on product, facility, and lifecycle stage.
- So, if there are gaps, my recommendation is to initiate a CAPA and manage the gaps through the CAPA process.
- If there are no gaps, then whoever owns your QMS did a really nice job and you should go shake their hand and say "thank you" because they have the most difficult job at your company and they never get any thanks for it. Seriously.

(6) Content

Next: Complete a Gap Assessment

The Quality Manual

Define the Product and the Product Phase

Define all regulations applicable to the product, phase of the product, and the facility used to manufacture the product.

Gap Assessment → Gaps? —Yes→ Manage through CAPA → THE END

No

(7) What to say…

Effective Policies & Procedure
 	
  • Effective Policies & Procedures represent the CONTROL of the QMS.
  • Hopefully you have some kind of document hierarchy like this (Content Part 2)

(7) Content Part 1

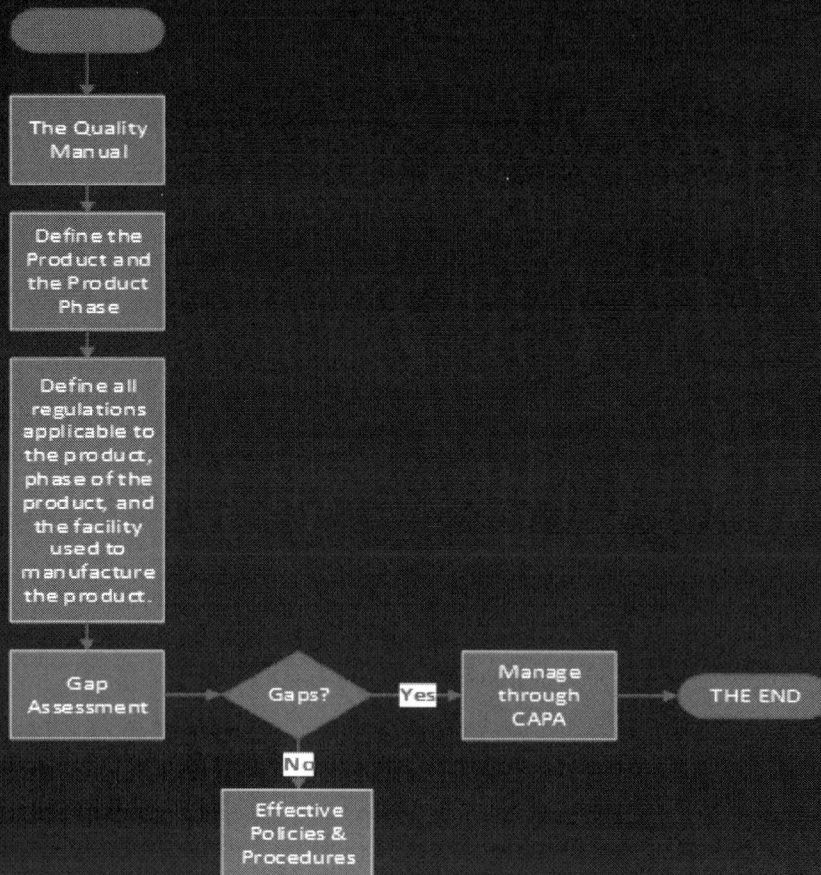

Effective Policies & Procedures

Figure 1 – QMS Document Hierarchy

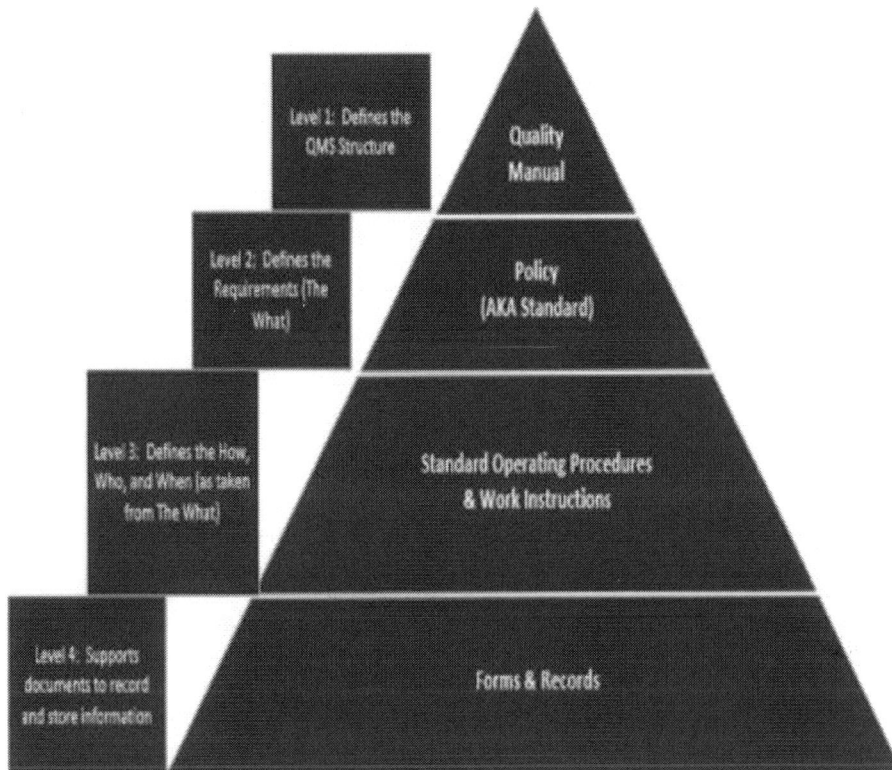

Level 1: Defines the QMS Structure — Quality Manual

Level 2: Defines the Requirements (The What) — Policy (AKA Standard)

Level 3: Defines the How, Who, and When (as taken from The What) — Standard Operating Procedures & Work Instructions

Level 4: Supports documents to record and store information — Forms & Records

(8) What to say...

Instilling Quality…

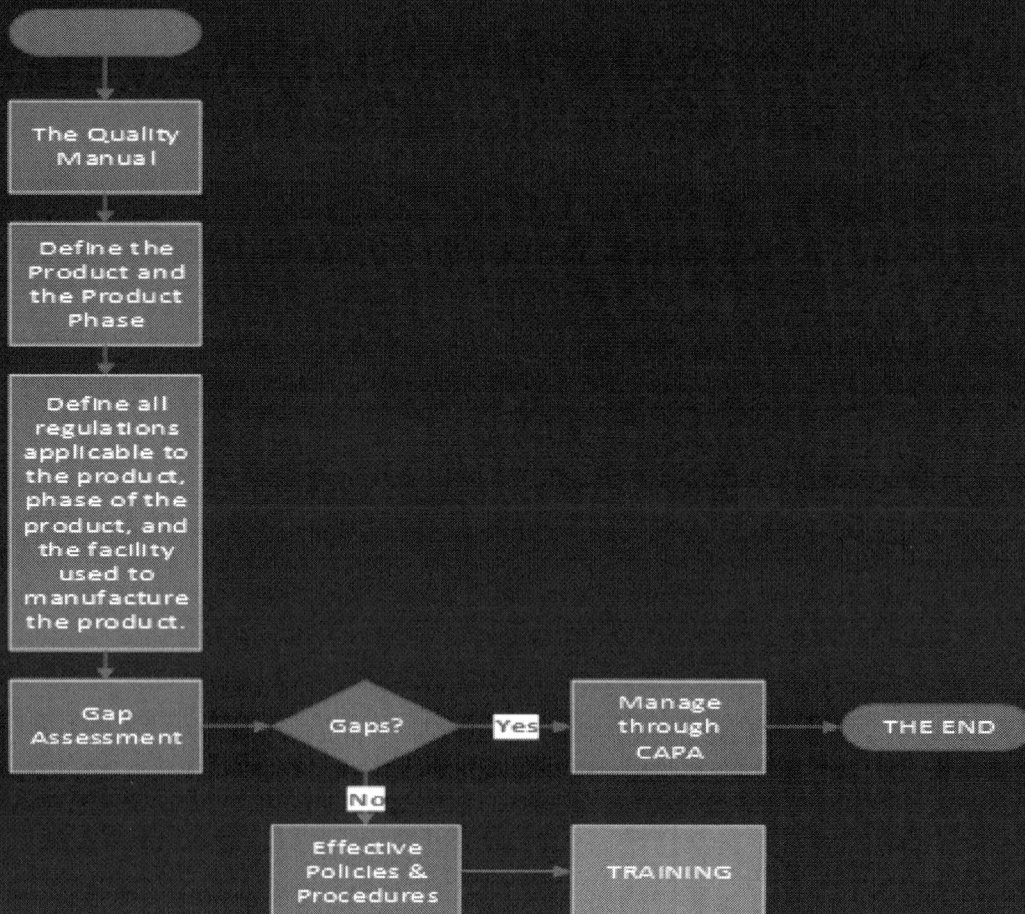

- In my Quality by Delitala Volume 4 book, which is aptly titled, Solving Problems Like a Pro, I tell a story about when I was the head of Training how alarming it was to me that everyone forgets the quality system of Training when they're planning for anything.
- I would argue that Training is how quality is instilled. Pharma companies need a modern approach to training so that it is effective in instilling quality into the full of the organization.

(8) Content

Instilling Quality...

```
[          ]
    │
    ▼
The Quality
  Manual
    │
    ▼
Define the
Product and
the Product
   Phase
    │
    ▼
Define all
regulations
applicable to
the product,
phase of the
product, and
the facility
used to
manufacture
the product.
    │
    ▼
    Gap          ──►  ◇ Gaps? ◇ ──Yes──►  Manage     ──►  THE END
Assessment                                through
                         │                 CAPA
                         No
                         │
                         ▼
                    Effective      ──►  TRAINING
                    Policies &
                    Procedures
```

(9) What to say...

Instilling Quality cont...

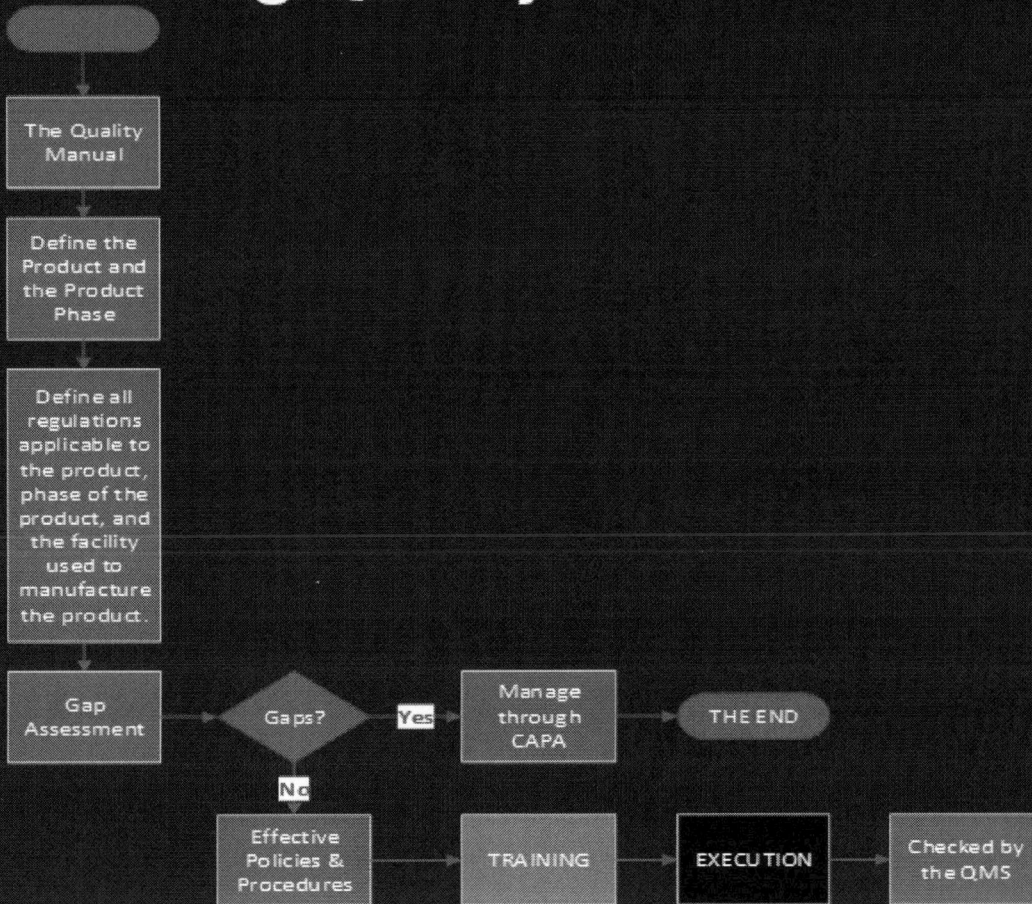

- Then, Execution of tasks occur, which has quality oversight, and checked and maintained by the Quality Management System.
- And that's how you implement, instill, and ensure continuous improvement of quality.
- But, I'm forgetting something extremely significant to this process.
- And if you're a good quality partner, this occurs in parallel to this process but does feed the process at about the gap assessment stage.

(9) Content

Instilling Quality cont...

```
The Quality Manual
        ↓
Define the Product and the Product Phase
        ↓
Define all regulations applicable to the product, phase of the product, and the facility used to manufacture the product.
        ↓
Gap Assessment → Gaps? → Yes → Manage through CAPA → THE END
                   ↓
                  No
                   ↓
Effective Policies & Procedures → TRAINING → EXECUTION → Checked by the QMS
```

(10)	What to say...

Do not forget about the business requirements...

- This is where I get my reputation for being somewhat of a rebel in quality.
- I promote the idea that best business practices equate to a high degree of quality.
- It has to.
- These two concepts (business & quality) must be married in order to run a successful business.
- Now, how do you that.
- I define this in QbDelitala Volume 4. Next slide.

(10)	Content

Do not forget about the business requirements...

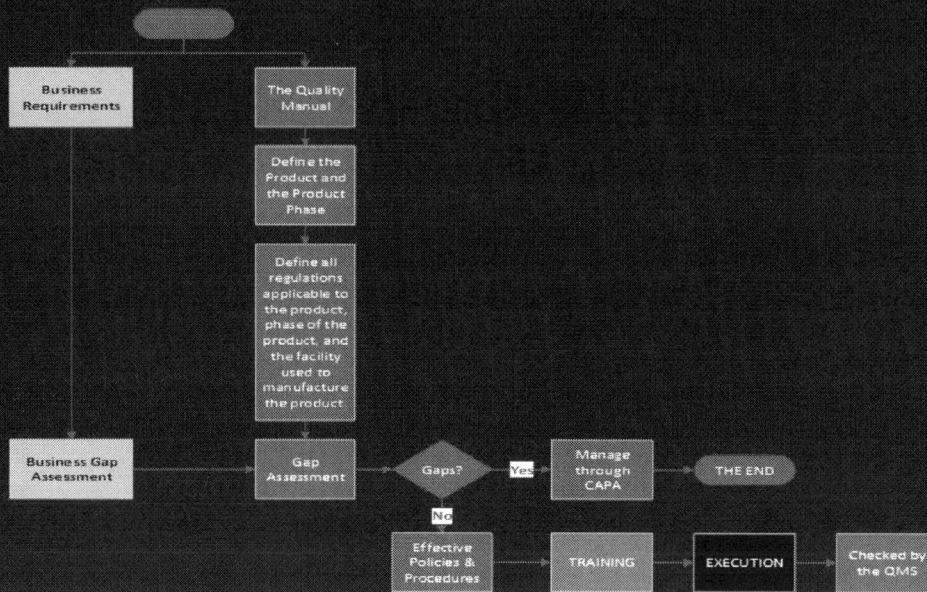

(11)	What to say…

Present the slide

(11)	Content

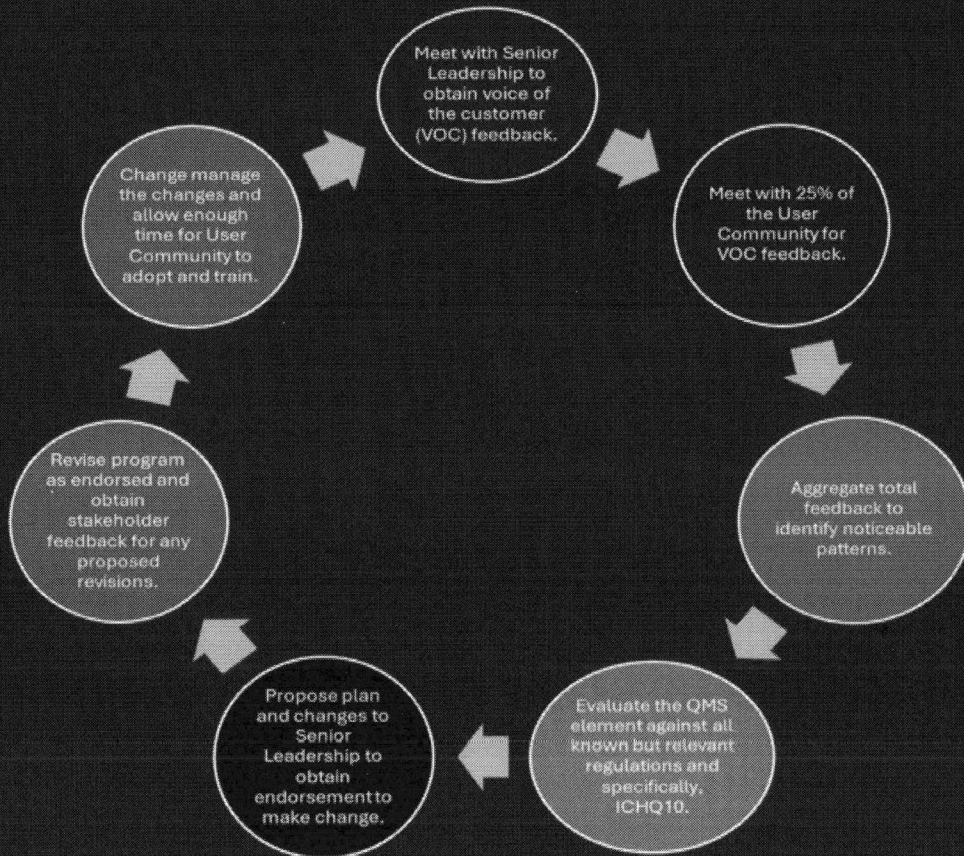

Obtaining business requirements…

- Meet with Senior Leadership to obtain voice of the customer (VOC) feedback.
- Meet with 25% of the User Community for VOC feedback.
- Aggregate total feedback to identify noticeable patterns.
- Evaluate the QMS element against all known but relevant regulations and specifically, ICHQ10.
- Propose plan and changes to Senior Leadership to obtain endorsement to make change.
- Revise program as endorsed and obtain stakeholder feedback for any proposed revisions.
- Change manage the changes and allow enough time for User Community to adopt and train.

(12)	What to say...

Present the slide

(12)	Content

Voice of the Customer...

Voice of the Customer Feedback	
Appreciate Inquiry	Continuous Improvement
What's working well?	If there was one thing to change immediately, what would it be and why?

(13)	What to say...

Present the slide

(14)	Content

Putting it all together...

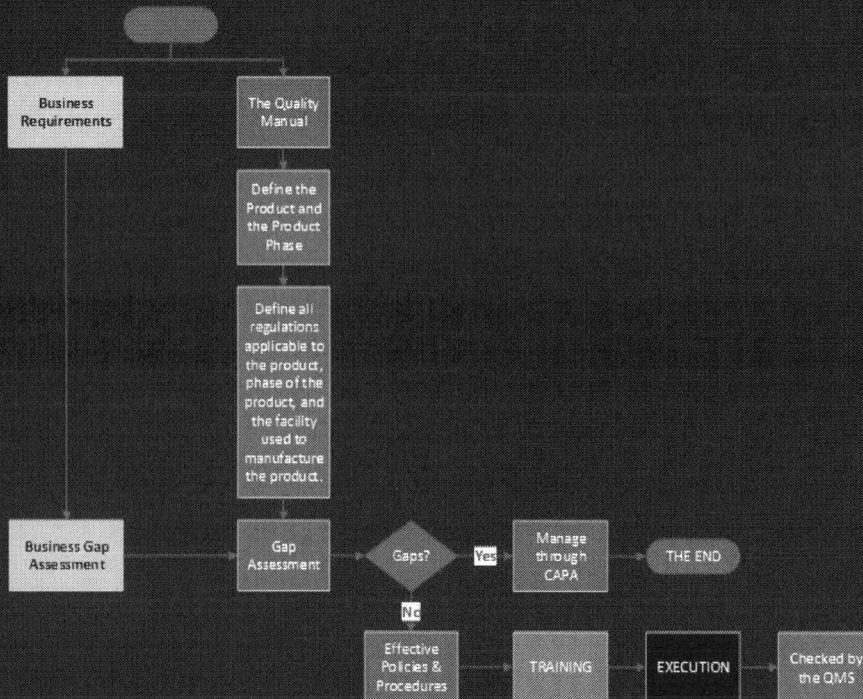

- Business Requirements
- The Quality Manual
- Define the Product and the Product Phase
- Define all regulations applicable to the product, phase of the product, and the facility used to manufacture the product.
- Business Gap Assessment
- Gap Assessment
- Gaps? — Yes → Manage through CAPA → THE END
- No → Effective Policies & Procedures → TRAINING → EXECUTION → Checked by the QMS

Appendix 3
Evoking a Quality of Presence (Thank you Lindsay B!)

INSTRUCTIONS

1. Focus on breath: Stand upright, focusing on your breath. Inhale up and out of the top of your head, lengthening your spine as you straighten and uplift your posture. Slowly take twice as long to exhale down your front all the way into the earth, softening your jaw and shoulders as you do.

2. Relate to Gravity: Feel the weight of your body and the weight of your arms pulling your shoulders away from your ears, and relax the tension in your jaw. Allow gravity to settle you into your personal space and onto the earth.

3. Balance personal space: Ask yourself what is the size of my personal space? Think about your personal space forming a bubble around you. Add a color to the space inside the bubble. Expand your personal space. Ask yourself if your personal space feels balanced around you and expand it to fill out the room.

4. Evoke a quality: Your quality represents something you want to cultivate in yourself. This is a process of inquiry with yourself. Ask: "If there were a little more___ (ease, confidence, compassion, etc) in my body, what would that be like? If there were 5% more of that quality, what would that feel like? Where do I notice that quality in my body?"

Appendix 4
The Marketing Materials in the Order to Present Them In (You're welcome!)

The Decision Making Model

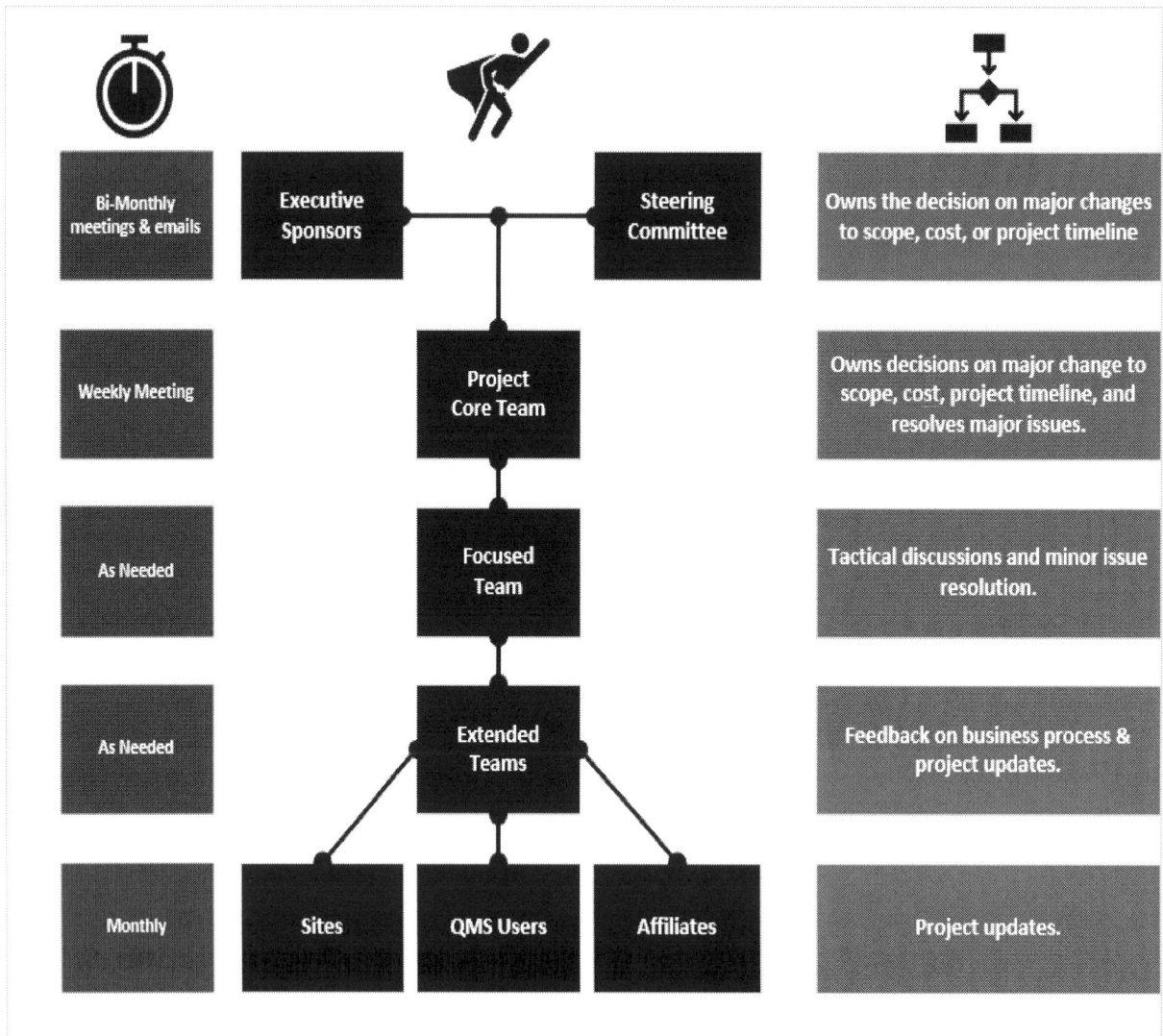

Roles & Responsibilities

Estimated Time Commitment

Focused Team Time Estimate
- Anticipate 25% of time per module (10 hours / week) for the entirety of the project.

Extended Team Time Estimate
- Anticipate 10-20% of time per module (4-8 hours / week) for the entirety of the project.

Other Considerations
- We generally know **only** 6-8 weeks out what major activities we'll be participating in.
- Most of us are in zoom – we are attempting to be more face to face.
- Travel must be approved by VP of Quality.
- We know this is not your day-job and that you'll have Site work in parallel.
- Designate an appropriate back up when appropriate given your priorities – onboard them!

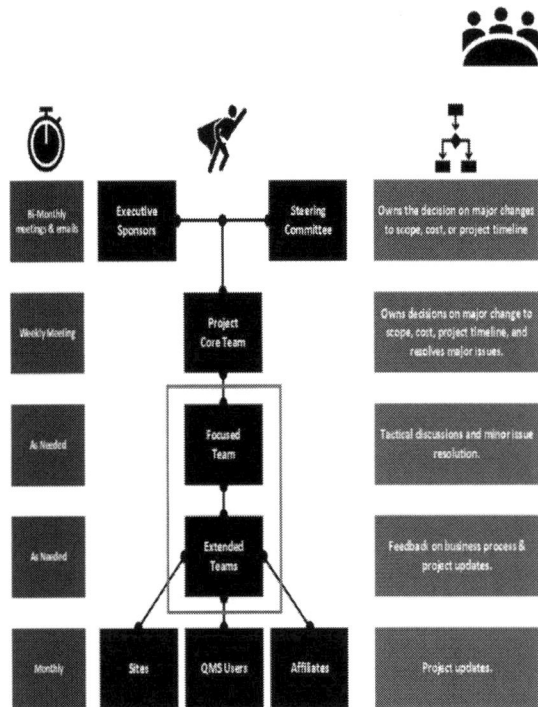

Project Business Leads & Focused Leads

- 100% dedicated.
- Responsible for leading the implementation roll-out at sites across all in scope modules per defined and approved phases.
- Serve as the single point of contact and change agent for their defined entity.
- Identify and recruit extended leads.
- Track revisions to controlled documents from their entity.
- Establish entity specific user requirements with justifications for user requirements that are additional or in conflict with Parent company requirements.
- ID user community and prepare community for Parent company training expectations.
- Communicate updates per communication plan.
- Communicate with entity leadership towards the end of resource allocation and support.
- Responsible for successful change adoption through expositions and roadshows.

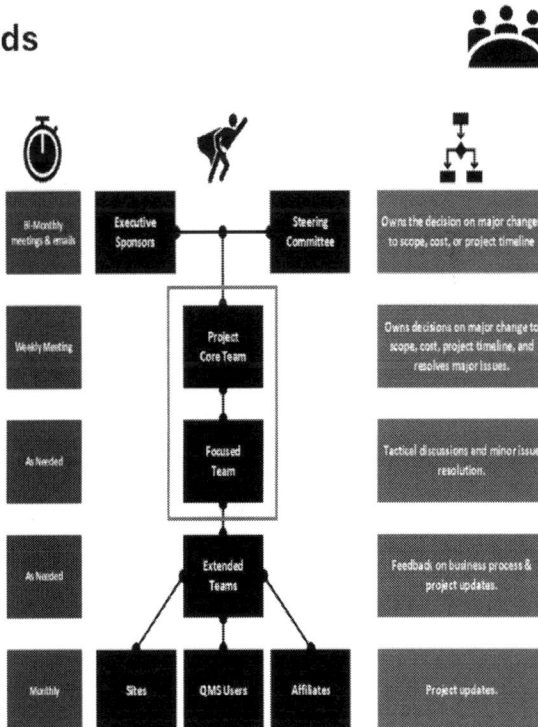

Focused Lead Global Program Owner Responsibilities

Focused Lead GPO Responsibilities

- Responsible for the implementation of the module.
- Drives alignment of the business process with site process owners with an enterprise mindset first and always.
- Supports effective meetings; deescalates conflict.
- The decision maker for the module.
- Leads communication efforts at the site level specifically with site leadership and all module stakeholders.
- Partners with Organization Change Management to ensure communicates are right given known business preferences.
- Partners with computerized system team to address configuration challenges.
- Assists with training development.

Figure 1 – Project Decision Making Model

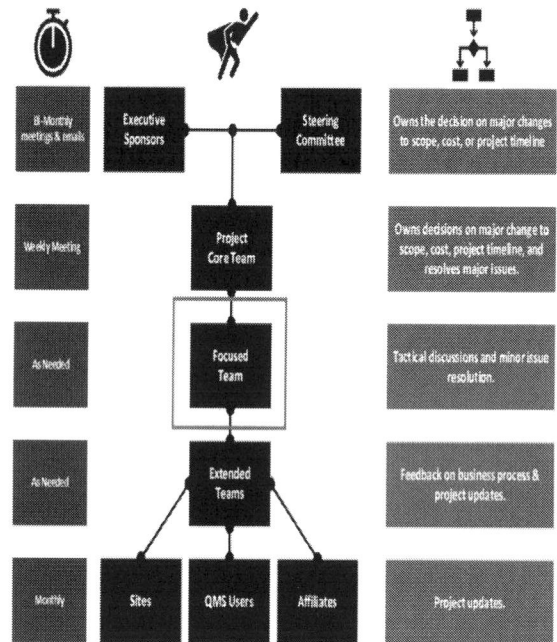

Bi-Monthly meetings & emails	Executive Sponsors — Steering Committee	Owns the decision on major changes to scope, cost, or project timeline
Weekly Meeting	Project Core Team	Owns decisions on major change to scope, cost, project timeline, and resolves major issues.
As Needed	Focused Team	Tactical discussions and minor issue resolution.
As Needed	Extended Teams	Feedback on business process & project updates.
Monthly	Sites QMS Users Affiliates	Project updates.

Focused Lead Responsibilities

• Supports modules of responsibility and evangelizes the to-be system to the sites for adoption. • Supports decisions for the enterprise, the site, and the function. • When delegating work, ensure a thorough onboarding plan to minimize business disruption.	• Actively participate in workshops to provide business preferences and practices, context, verify controlled documents, and complete all workshop pre-work and actual work. • Provide centralized and aggregate feedback on solutions during each process exercise phase based on process exercise scope. • Provide centralized and aggregate feedback on functional use cases, operational challenges, and the user experience. • Identify risks and propose mitigation actions.	• Work with the extended team during reviews and assessments to help gather feedback in the scope of the process exercise. • Act as a change agent to communicate decisions of the project team to sites and functional areas. • Collect and provide feedback on controlled documents including procedures and training. • Participate as a subject matter expert in the system during testing and process exercises. • Support the development of user community training.

Extended Team Responsibilities

Extended Team Responsibilities
- Coordinates with the Focus Team Lead for their site or functional area.
- Participates in Process Exercise hands on testing.
- Collects and provides feedback to the Focus Team Representative on the solution at each system iteration including any stakeholder needs based on business use cases.
- Acts as change agent for their organization, site, or functional area.
- Assigns back up and onboards them if/when they're going to be out of the office.

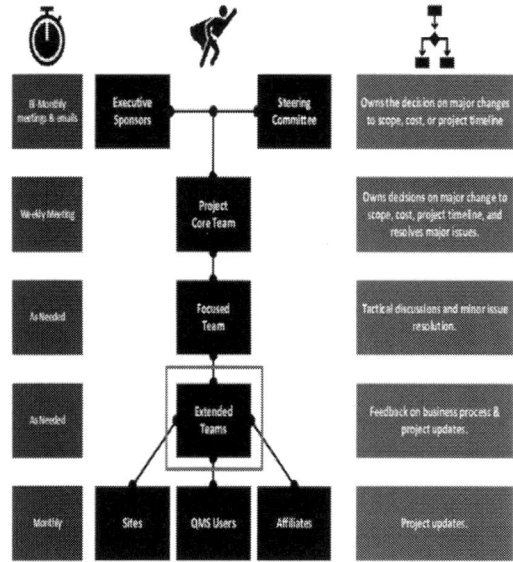

Figure 1 – Project Decision Making Model

Guiding Principles & Business Drivers

The Future is Now

The Vision
- A simple, enterprise globally facing and integrated system that is user focused, enables data driven insights for focused decisions, and adaptable to the ever-evolving needs of the business.

Guiding Principles
- Keep it **SIMPLE** to achieve scalability and compliance
- Focus on **USER EXPERIENCE**, fit for purpose and ease of use
- Design for **AGILITY** and **ADAPTABILITY** to evolving business needs
- Be **BOLD** and **INNOVATIVE** with the future in mind
- Focus on use of **DATA TO DRIVE INSIGHTS** in the vein of continuous improvement
- **ENTERPRISE & ALIGNMENT MINDSETS**

Primary Business Drivers for a Modern QMS

Functionality
- Support evolving QMS needs by replacing legacy systems which are complex, inflexible and at end-of-life.

Knowledge & Intelligence
- Leverage "deep learning" to identify risks that are not easily identified. Real time data visualization.

Process Automation
- Reduce repetitive data entry, manual steps, and inefficiencies through automation.

Information Connectivity
- Integrated systems improve efficiency by connecting product, regulatory, and quality information.

Usability
- Simple and intuitive user interface to improve the user experience.

External Access & Collaboration
- Contract partners can directly enter data and collaborate with Company to address various quality event workstreams.

Just-in-Time Training
- Expanded use of just-in-time training and digital adoption tools to ensure targeted training to users.

The VEEVA Process

High Level Implementation Timeline – Key Milestones

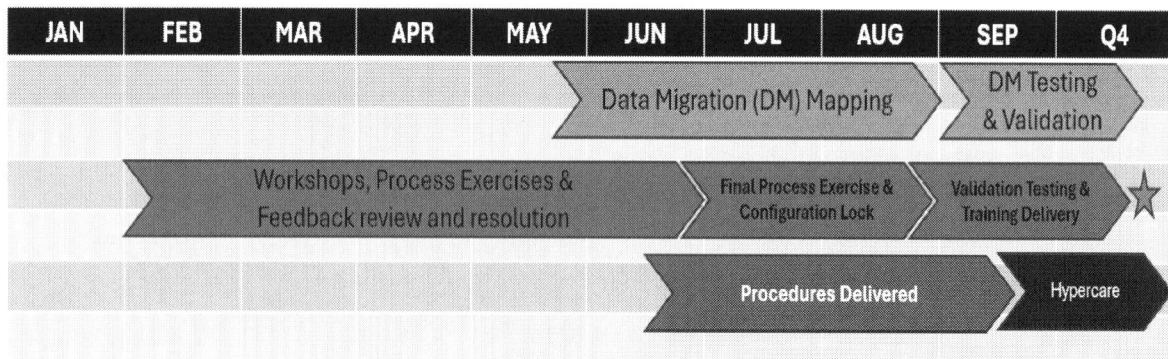

JAN	FEB	MAR	APR	MAY	JUN	JUL	AUG	SEP	Q4
					Data Migration (DM) Mapping			DM Testing & Validation	
	Workshops, Process Exercises & Feedback review and resolution					Final Process Exercise & Configuration Lock		Validation Testing & Training Delivery	
						Procedures Delivered			Hypercare

⭐ Go-Live

Project Scope by Phase, Year, and Modules

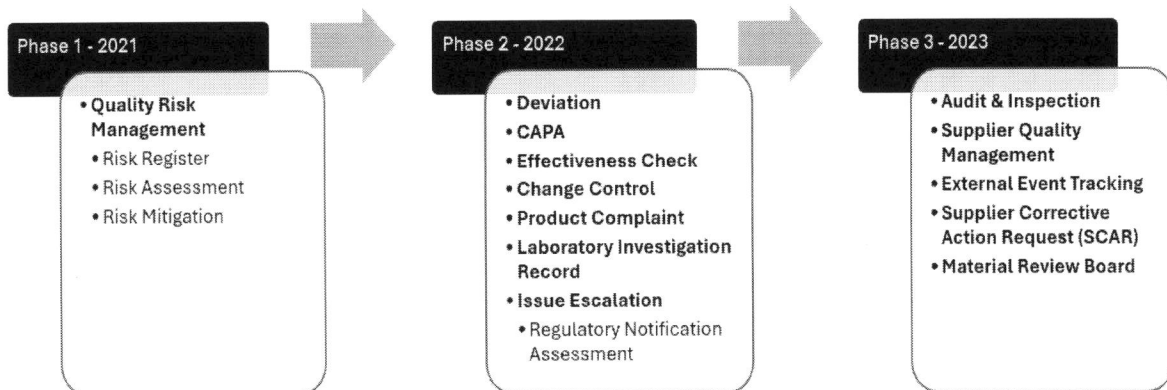

Phase 1 - 2021
- **Quality Risk Management**
  - Risk Register
  - Risk Assessment
  - Risk Mitigation

Phase 2 - 2022
- **Deviation**
- **CAPA**
- **Effectiveness Check**
- **Change Control**
- **Product Complaint**
- **Laboratory Investigation Record**
- **Issue Escalation**
  - Regulatory Notification Assessment

Phase 3 - 2023
- **Audit & Inspection**
- **Supplier Quality Management**
- **External Event Tracking**
- **Supplier Corrective Action Request (SCAR)**
- **Material Review Board**

Note: The **bolded** font represents the parent module with a subset of unbolded font with represents an associated child record. Ex: **Issue Escalation** is the parent with the Regulatory Notification Assessment being a child to the parent.

The Process Exercise Methodology

1. **Hands on Evaluation**
   1. The Process Exercise is based on a combination of the delivered application and enterprise-specific requirements.
2. **Feedback Gathered**
   1. Feedback is entered in the Process Exercise feedback recording tool (like a SmartSheet) and is reviewed by the Focused Team.
3. **Process Exercise Review**
   1. Daily office hours to support teams with questions/concerns/feedback/errors.
   2. Feedback is actively monitored with updates and status reviews to determine acceptance or justification for not implementing.
4. **Configuration Updates**
   1. The configuration team will configure all agreed upon changes or fixes.
   2. Changes are socialized through office hours and other daily communication mediums.

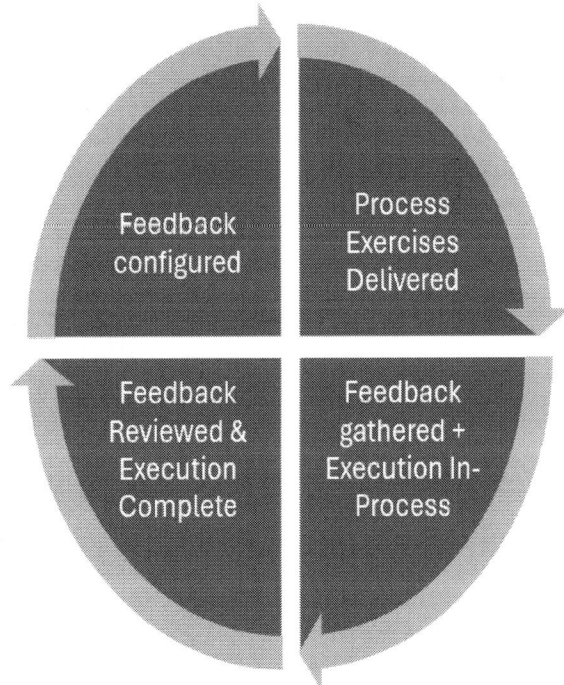

Feedback configured → Process Exercises Delivered → Feedback gathered + Execution In-Process → Feedback Reviewed & Execution Complete

The Sprint Format

- WEEK 1 – Requirements
- WEEK 2 – Configuration
- WEEK 3 – Process Exercises
- WEEK 4 – Feedback & Configuration

MON	TUE	WED	THU	FRI
Deviation CAPA	Change Control	Product Complaints	LIRs	Issue Escalation

The 4x4 Sprint Format

FEB2025

S	M	T	W	T	F	S
	D/C	CC	PC	LIR	IE	1
2	3	4	5	6	7	8
9	10	11	12	13	14	15
16	17	18	19	20	21	22
23	24	25	26	27	28	

MAR2025

S	M	T	W	T	F	S
	D/C	CC	PC	LIR	IE	1
2	3	4	5	6	7	8
9	10	11	12	13	14	15
16	17	18	19	20	21	22
23	24	25	26	27	28	29
30	31					

APR2025

S	M	T	W	T	F	S
	D/C	CC	PC	LIR	IE	
		1	2	3	4	5
6	7	8	9	10	11	12
13	14	15	16	17	18	19
20	21	22	23	24	25	26
27	28	29	30			

MAY2025

S	M	T	W	T	F	S
	D/C	CC	PC	LIR	IE	
				1	2	3
4	5	6	7	8	9	10
11	12	13	14	15	16	17
18	19	20	21	22	23	24
25	26	27	28	29	30	31

JUN2025

S	M	T	W	T	F	S
	D/C	CC	PC	LIR	IE	
1	2	3	4	5	6	7
8	9	10	11	12	13	14
15	16	17	18	19	20	21
22	23	24	25	26	27	28
29	30					

- Sprint 1 – System, Life Cycle, States, and Key Data Fields.
- Sprint 2 – Field Rules & Workflow Automation.
- Sprint 3 – Security logic, Roles, Permissions, and Formatted Outputs
- Sprint 4 – Reports & Dashboards

- Requirement Gathering Workshops
- Configuration & Touchpoint Demonstrations
- Process Exercises Released & Feedback
- Evaluate and address feedback

Deviation Module Deep Dive Preparation Leading up to Go-Live

User Community Insights:
- 20% of the Qualified User Community is active in Agile-QMS over the past 12 months.
- There are 500 Deviation Owners
- There are 185 Quality Approvers
- Assumption: All 685 users will access and therefore transition to the new QMS Deviation module.

New Role – Functional Area Approver – What do we know today?
- The role will be optional for Major/Critical deviations.
- The role will be optional because after reviewing the data for Major and Critical deviations, the majority of them ended up being for incoming material out of specifications which is a deviation type that cannot be corrected. The thought is that rigorous resources do not need to be applied.
- For all other Major/Critical deviations with root causes of Manpower, Machinery, Method, or Mother Nature, the FAA option must be exercised.
- The idea of the FAA is that this will be a centralized function limiting access to the experienced few.

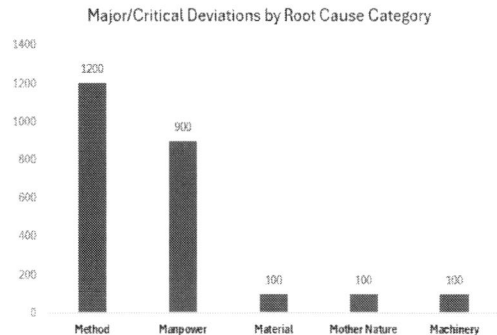

Major/Critical Deviations by Root Cause Category

Category	Value
Method	1200
Manpower	900
Material	100
Mother Nature	100
Machinery	100

What are CLINICAL-CA-TCF preferences?

Deviation Module Deep Dive Preparation Leading up to Go-Live

FAA Option 1	FAA Option 2	FAA Option 3
Centralize the FA Approver per department	All Current Managers of existing User Community to have FA Approver Access	Hybrid of Options 1 & 2 at the discretion of the Site Leadership Team (SLT)
• The idea is that there is one primary FA Approver per department. • This person is like a Head of their area or they are the primary delegate for the department. • They tend to have the most experience, are responsible for scheduling, usually a manager of managers.	• ~300 Managers would require training for FA Approver role. • Based on data insights of the existing user community, although these staff would be trained and have access it feels like they would hardly ever use the role.	To be socialized
• This option means there are very few FA Approvers which means although a new role, it is limited and requires little training. • This means the "right" approvers are approving Major/Critical deviations when the option is required or exercised to do so. • **GPO Recommendation Based on Data Insights: 1 primary FAA and one backup delegate FAA per department.**	• This is a decentralized model and is discouraged because the idea is an oversight and accountability model per ICHQ10.	To be socialized

The company will need to decide who / which option is best all data and all things considered

Deviation Module Deep Dive Preparation Leading up to Go-Live

New Role: Deviation Initiator
- Deviation Initiators start deviations when first observed and then later transfer to an Owner.
- This role has been requested by the business, namely manufacturing, to gain efficiencies in day-to-day processing of deviation records especially during shift changes.
- In Agile, one must go through comprehensive training to gain access as an Owner because Initiator is not a role in Agile and the role cannot be implemented in Agile due to it being antiquated.
- In Veeva, the Initiator will require less training because the role only allows the record to be progressed to classification. At classification, the record must be transferred to an Owner.
- There were ~7400 deviations initiated 01JAN2021-31MAY2022.
  - **~3900 Minor (which is where this role adds the greatest value proposition)**
  - ~2300 Major
  - ~1100 Critical

The company (each site) will need a decision on who will be an initiator.

Deviation Module Deep Dive Preparation Leading up to Go-Live

Demonstrating How Deviation Connects to other QMS Modules
- The below chevron map depicts parent child associations while coexisting in two QMSs.

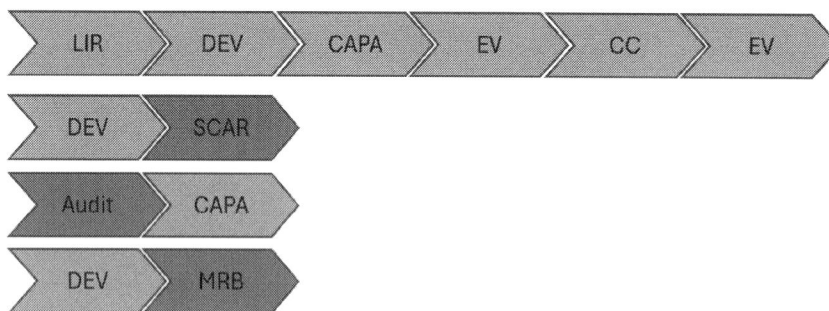

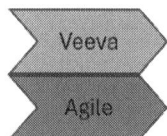

There are three examples where the company will have to be tolerant of existing in two QMSs.

Do the Global Owners know and will those system SOPs require revision?

Deviation Module Deep Dive Preparation Leading up to Go-Live

Document Strategy Implementation Planning

- Controlled documents for deviation will have to consider coexisting in two QMSs.
- FACT: The current program documents are system specific to Agile-QMS.
- FACT: The Agile-QMS Deviation Module will be decommissioned 90 days after going live with Veeva.
- FACT: Parent-company will implement system agnostic controlled documents will be effective on go-live.
- FACT: Child-company has immunotherapy specific requirements and will maintain global documents.
- FACT: New Parent & Child Global Training Curricula will be required (obsolete the old).

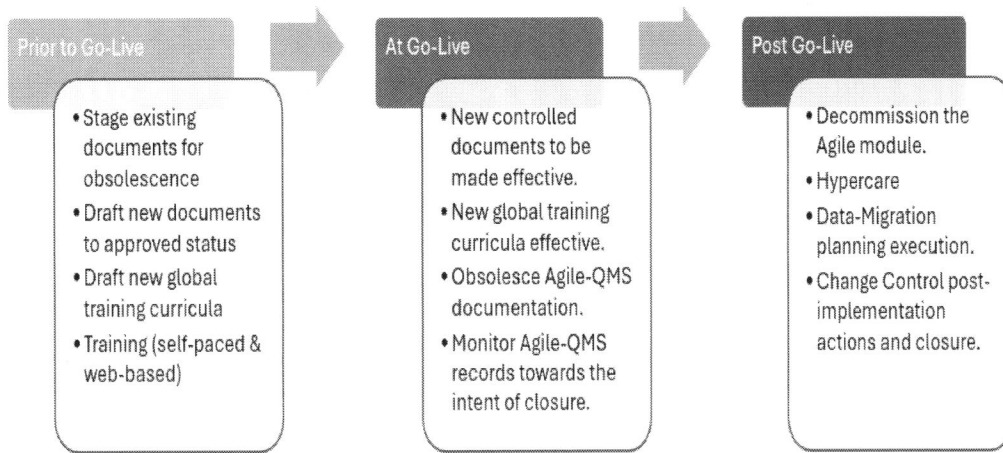

Prior to Go-Live	At Go-Live	Post Go-Live
• Stage existing documents for obsolescence • Draft new documents to approved status • Draft new global training curricula • Training (self-paced & web-based)	• New controlled documents to be made effective. • New global training curricula effective. • Obsolesce Agile-QMS documentation. • Monitor Agile-QMS records towards the intent of closure.	• Decommission the Agile module. • Hypercare • Data-Migration planning execution. • Change Control post-implementation actions and closure.

Deviation Module Deep Dive Preparation Leading up to Go-Live

What else does Deviation require?

- Validated reports on record and object statuses
- Dashboards representative of quality management review statuses
- Quick Reference guides on reports and queries to generate lists for inspections (Inspectors).
- Dashboards representative of manufacturing work center teams (nice to have).
- **REQUIRED:** Disposition Report (Report generated to determine status of product impact assessments)
- **REQUIRED: Disposition Report – Final Product Disposition**

CAPA/EV Module Deep Dive Preparation Leading up to Go-Live

CAPA	Effectiveness Verification (EV)
450 CAPA Owners	600 EV Owners (the delta is that the access is shared with CC)
150 Quality Approvers	300 Quality Approvers

- Veeva is an object based platform. This means it has a parent record with objects associated to it.
- The parent record is known as a Quality Event (QE).
- So, each parent record starts off with QE, then a dash, then a number and the meta-data is what sets is apart as a stand alone record.
- Example: QE-0001 and the QMS Record = deviation.
- This is fundamentally different than Agile-QMS.
- In Agile-QMS each record is quality event.
- This is critical to highlight right now because EVs are parent records in Agile-QMS.
- EVs will be objects associated to a parent in Veeva.
- In Agile-QMS, EV access is obtained when you are trained on CAPA or Change Control or both.
- In Veeva-QMS, EV access is provided when you are trained on CAPA or Change Control.
- In Veeva-QMS, EV is one object that can be associated to any Parent Record. It cannot be a stand alone record (like we have right now).

• 100 CAPAs per quarter	• 30 EVs per quarter
• Only 20% of the population is active.	• Only 10% of the population is active

CAPA/EV Module Deep Dive Preparation Leading up to Go-Live

Sources of CAPA and Effectiveness Verification	
CAPA	Effectiveness Verification (EV)
17 Sources	5 Sources
Examples...	Examples...

CAPA Examples	EV Examples
• Annual Product Review	• CAPA
• BPDR	• Change Control
• Internal Audit	• Deviation
• Gap Assessment	• SCAR
• Document Control Revision Gap Assessment	• Risk Management
• Deviation	
• Root Cause Analysis	
• Product Complaint	
• Quality Management Review	
• Change Control	
• Risk Management	

The controlled documents associated to these sources will be evaluated to determine if they should be revised

CAPA/EV Module Deep Dive Preparation Leading up to Go-Live

FAA Option 1	FAA Option 2
• The idea is that there is one primary FA Approver per department. • This person is like a Head of their area or they are the primary delegate for the department. • They tend to have the most experience, are responsible for scheduling, usually a manager of managers.	• ~300 Managers would require training for FA Approver role. • Based on data insights of the existing user community, although these staff would be trained and have access it feels like they would hardly ever use the role.
• This option means there are very few FA Approvers which means although a new role, it is limited and requires little training. • **GPO Recommendation Based on Data Insights: 1 primary FAA and one backup delegate FAA per department.**	• This is a decentralized model and is discouraged because the idea is an oversight and accountability model per ICHQ10.

The company will need to decide who / which option is best all data and all things considered

CAPA/EV Module Deep Dive Preparation Leading up to Go-Live

Document Strategy Implementation Planning
- Controlled documents for CAPA/EV will have to consider coexisting in two QMSs.
- FACT: The current program documents are system specific to Agile-QMS.
- FACT: The Agile-QMS CAPA/EV Module will be decommissioned 90 days after going live with Veeva.
- FACT: Parent-company will implement system agnostic controlled documents effective on go-live.
- FACT: Child-company has immunotherapy specific requirements and will maintain global documents.
- FACT: New Parent & Child Global Training Curricula will be required (obsolete the old).

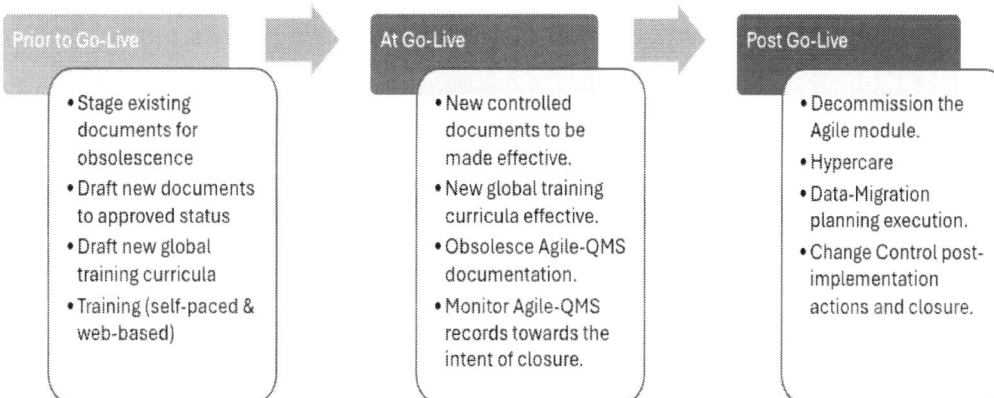

Prior to Go-Live
- Stage existing documents for obsolescence
- Draft new documents to approved status
- Draft new global training curricula
- Training (self-paced & web-based)

At Go-Live
- New controlled documents to be made effective.
- New global training curricula effective.
- Obsolesce Agile-QMS documentation.
- Monitor Agile-QMS records towards the intent of closure.

Post Go-Live
- Decommission the Agile module.
- Hypercare
- Data-Migration planning execution.
- Change Control post-implementation actions and closure.

Change Control Module Deep Dive Preparation Leading up to Go-Live

Change Control
400 Change Control Owners
200 Quality Approvers
500 Impact Assessors with 20 of them in Regulatory Affairs

- The company is growing – The number of change control is increasing as the company licenses more products and joins other jurisdictions.

Change Control Module Deep Dive Preparation Leading up to Go-Live

NEW: Initiator Role	Change Owner	NEW: FA Approver	Quality Approver
• New capability in the QMS with a Change Proposal Process. • Only Change Initiators will have the access to initiate a change proposal.	• Same as Agile-QMS.	• Required for all changes regardless of risk classification and regardless of the change being global or not global.	• Same as Agile-QMS.

FAA Option 1	FAA Option 2
• The idea is that there is one primary FA Approver per department. • This person is like a Head of their area or they are the primary delegate for the department. • They tend to have the most experience, are responsible for scheduling, usually a manager of managers.	• ~300 Managers would require training for FA Approver role.
• This option means there are very few FA Approvers which means although a new role, it is limited and requires little training. • **GPO Recommendation Based on Data Insights: 1 primary FAA and one backup delegate FAA per department.**	• This is a decentralized model and is discouraged because the idea is an oversight and accountability model per ICHQ10.

Change Control Module Deep Dive Preparation Leading up to Go-Live

Demonstrating How Change Control Connects to other QMS Modules
- The below chevron map depicts parent child associations while coexisting in two QMSs.

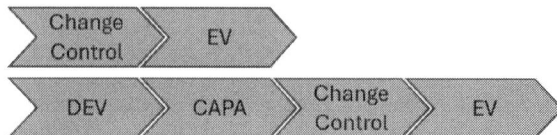

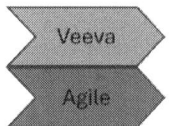

Change Control → EV

DEV → CAPA → Change Control → EV

Veeva • In the change space, all will be in one QMS.

Agile ? Do the Global Owners know and will those system SOPs require revision?

Change Control Module Deep Dive Preparation Leading up to Go-Live

Document Strategy Implementation Planning
- Controlled documents for CC will have to consider coexisting in two QMSs.
- FACT: The current program documents are system specific to Agile-QMS.
- FACT: The Agile-QMS CC Module will be decommissioned 90 days after going live with Veeva.
- FACT: Parent-company will implement system agnostic controlled documents effective on go-live.
- FACT: Child-company has immunotherapy specific requirements and will maintain global documents.
- FACT: New Parent & Child Global Training Curricula will be required (obsolete the old).

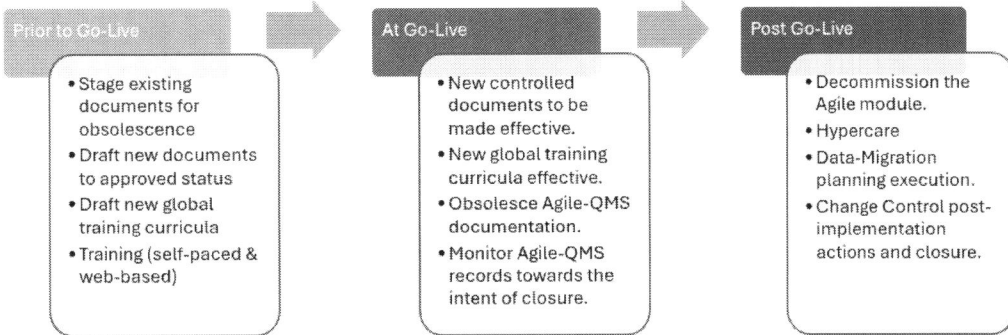

Prior to Go-Live
- Stage existing documents for obsolescence
- Draft new documents to approved status
- Draft new global training curricula
- Training (self-paced & web-based)

At Go-Live
- New controlled documents to be made effective.
- New global training curricula effective.
- Obsolesce Agile-QMS documentation.
- Monitor Agile-QMS records towards the intent of closure.

Post Go-Live
- Decommission the Agile module.
- Hypercare
- Data-Migration planning execution.
- Change Control post-implementation actions and closure.

Organizational Change Management

Organizational Change Management Adoption Strategy

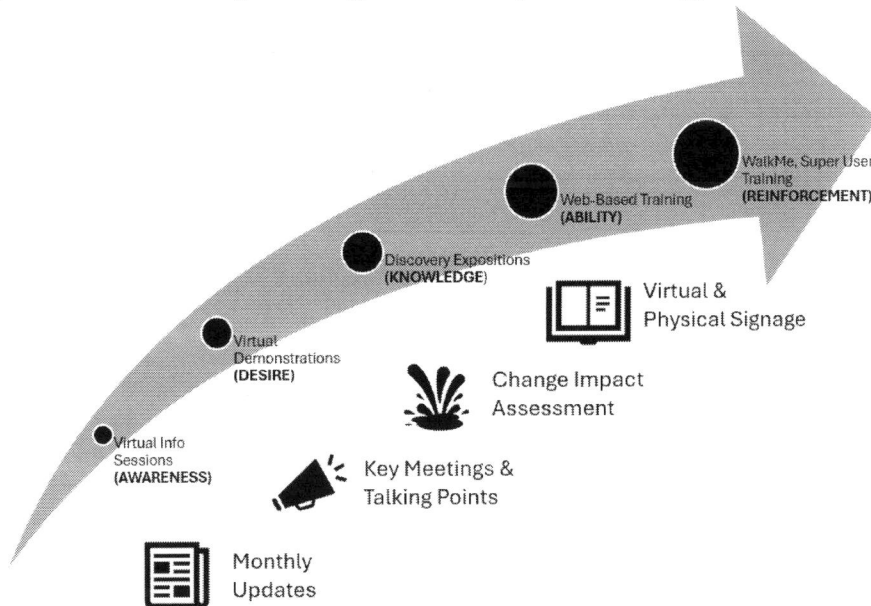

WalkMe, Super User Training (REINFORCEMENT)

Web-Based Training (ABILITY)

Discovery Expositions (KNOWLEDGE)

Virtual Demonstrations (DESIRE)

Virtual Info Sessions (AWARENESS)

Virtual & Physical Signage

Change Impact Assessment

Key Meetings & Talking Points

Monthly Updates

Hypercare Marketing Materials

Email Distribution List	Office Hours	MS Team's Channel	FAQs

Site-Specific Activities to Complete the Implementation

SITE-SPECIFIC TASKS							
Role Mapping by Module	Super User Training	Curriculum Management	Local Document Revisions	Create Reports & Views	Site Hypercare Support	Open Record Migration	Exposition Support

A few assumptions to consider with the tasks:

1. It is assumed that we will likely have the same training strategy as last year (mostly ILT and R/U).
2. There is a limited budget for travel.
3. All Leads from all Entities will be working together this year towards the alignment with the Parent company.
4. Many of the staff who need access to the Phase 3 modules most likely have some kind of access to Gvault QMS (so, it's not as big of a lift in Phase 3 as it was in Phase 2).

Note to the Reader: In my actual marketing materials I used the bubbles icon that you see next to the assumptions above. This is because our bubbles were popped in each of these categories. For example, we basically had an unlimited budget for Phase 2. And because we spent so much money on travel and expositions (I spent $24000 in Amsterdam alone!) we were told to come up with solutions where we spent no money!

0168081f-af38-471b-911d-f2f6475a30e7R01